imary Dictionary of
erfect Spelling

Christine Maxwell and Julia Rowlandson

Barrington Stoke

This edition published in Great Britain by Barrington Stoke Ltd, 18 Walker Street, Edinburgh, EH3 7LP

www.barringtonstoke.co.uk

ISBN 1-84299-401-8

Cover design by Latte Goldstein

Trademarks
Words in this dictionary which we believe to be trademarks have been acknowledged as such. The presence or absence of such acknowledgements should not be regarded as affecting the legal status of any trademark or proprietary name.

Typeset by GreenGate Publishing Services, Tonbridge TN9 2RN
Printed in Spain at Graficas Cems SL by arrangement with Associated Agencies Ltd, Oxford

Acknowledgements

I would like to thank the following people:

Christine Maxwell for having the original insight into creating a dictionary that can be easily used by poor spellers.

All the children who contributed misspellings which often in their opinion were how the words should be spelt!

My late father, David Driver, who tirelessly checked head words with me.

Ruth Paris for her patient editorial work and sense of humour.

Kate MacPhee and Joanna Craddock for their proof-reading skills.

Julia Rowlandson BA Hons, PGCE, Dip RSA, SpLD

Preface

To the Teacher

After the publication of the revised and updated *Dictionary of Perfect Spelling*, Barrington Stoke has had numerous requests for a Primary version.

In my work as Head of English in a school for boys with specific learning difficulties, I continually witnessed the frustrations of children trying to use a conventional dictionary to help with their spelling. More often or not they gave up and spelt the word phonically. In the *Primary Spelling Dictionary*, following Christine Maxwell's inspirational idea, they can do just this.

But when they check their phonic spelling, if they find the word in red, it is wrong and beside it they will find the correct spelling in black.

For example: eny   any

They can then locate the correct spelling and check any derivatives.

For example: any ~body ~how ~one

any ~thing ~way ~where

The tilde(~) tells the user to just add on the ending to the root word.

Irregular plurals are given.

For example: wolf   wolves

Verb endings are given in full.

For example: fly [flies flying flew flown]

Comparative adjectives are spelt out.

For example: funny funnier funniest

If they have difficulty finding a word, there are hints as to where else to look.

For example: Under ci you will find

Check out
si as well

I have included some useful spelling rules which need to be taught and learnt. I found Gill Cotterell's Phonic Reference cards published by LDA an excellent resource.

To the Speller!

The English language is very hard for the person who hates spelling because groups of letters can make more than one sound. Even spell checkers find it hard! However, 86% of words do stick to rules and the tips on pages v to vii are there to help you. We call the other 14% of words 'irregular' because they do not follow rules or patterns and you need to find ways to remember them.
Pages viii to x will give you some ideas of ways to learn them.

We all need to spell words the same way to make sure that we can write what we want to say and so everyone who reads it can understand exactly what we mean.

Some Useful English Spelling Rules –
It does help to learn them!!

1. Remember vowels (a e i o u) can make a short sound or a long sound (like their name).
   For example ā as in ape [long – its name], ă as in apple [short – its sound].
   'y' sometimes acts as a vowel as well, e.g. 'cry' and 'rhythm'.
2. Have fun with words! Learn to build words from the root word, use **prefixes** (bits you add on the front) and **suffixes** (bits you add on the end).
   For example: stand, <u>under</u>stand, understand<u>ing</u>, <u>mis</u><u>under</u>stand**ing**
3. 'q' always has 'u' with it and is written 'qu' like in 'quiz' and 'question'.
4. No word ends in 'v' except 'spiv' (a flashy man). Often 'e' comes after 'v' to prop it up like in 'active' and 'native'.

5. No word ends in 'j'.

6. Never write a 'k' before a 't'. Always write 'ct' as in 'fact' and 'direct'.

7. No English word ends in 'i'.
    Watch out for rule breakers: taxi (short for taxicab) and ski, spaghetti and macaroni (but they aren't English!).

8. The 'ee' sound at the end of a word is mostly spelt 'y'.
    Watch out for rule breakers: coffee and committee!

9. Double 'l' 'f' and 's' after a single vowel in a short word, e.g. spell, boss, stiff, puff. Watch out for rule breakers: us, bus, gas, if, of, this, yes, plus, nil, pal!

10. Add 's' to make a regular plural as in 'cat - cats'.

11. Add 'es' to make a plural if the word has a hissing ending like: 's - buses, x - foxes, sh - brushes, ch - churches, ss – fusses.

12. If a word ends in one 'f', change it to 'v' and add 'es' to make the plural.
    For example: leaf ➤ leav ➤ leaves, wolf ➤ wolv ➤ wolves.

    Watch out for rule breakers: dwarfs, chiefs, roofs!

13. For most words that end in 'o', add 'es' to make the plural. For example: potato + es = potatoes.

    Watch out for rule breakers: pianos, solos, Eskimos!

14. The prefix 'all' at the start of a word is only spelt with one 'l' – almost, altogther, also, already.

15. The suffixes 'full and till' at the end of the word only have one 'l' – helpful, until.

16. Remember the suffix to make an adverb is 'ly' NOT 'ley'!

17. Drop the final 'e' from the root word before adding a suffix that starts with a vowel. For example: move + ed = moved, like + ing = liking, drive + er = driver, muddle + ed = muddled.

18. If a word ends in a consonant + y, change the 'y' to 'i' before adding any ending except 'ing'. For example:
marry + es = marries, funny + ly = funnily.
BUT fly – ing = flying, carry - ing = carrying.

19. 'ck', 'dge', 'tch' are used after a short vowel (one that says its sound). For example: back, hedge, match.
Watch out for rule breakers: rich, much, such, which!

20. If a words ends in a single vowel and a single consonant always double the final consonant before adding a suffix that starts with a vowel.
For example: stop + ed = stopped, fat + er = fatter, hot + est = hottest, rob + ing = robbing.

21. 'ce', 'ci', 'cy' makes the /s/ sound.
For example: centre, circle, cycle.

22. 'ge', 'gi', 'gy' makes the /j/ sound.
For example: gentle, giant, gym.
Watch out for rule breakers: get, begin, girl, give, gear, geese, gift, girth!

23. 'i' comes before 'e' except after c, but not when it sounds like /ā/ as in 'neighbour' and 'weigh'.
Watch out for rule breakers: neither, foreign, seized, sovereign, forfeit!

Ways to Learn Spellings

Hear it 👂   See it 👁   Say it 👄   Do it ✋

To remember a spelling you must –

1. Think about the word that you are trying to learn and make sure you understand what it means.
2. Divide it into syllables (chunks). You can find where they are by putting your hand under your chin and counting how many times your chin goes down when you say the word.
    For example: Sat/ur/day = 3 syllables. Note that each syllable must have a vowel. It can sometimes be 'y'.
3. Talk about which parts of the word are hard to spell and highlight them.
4. Practise spelling the word at odd times, e.g. on the way to school, in the shower/bath, etc.
5. Learn other words with the same pattern and then they will be easier to remember. For example:
    few, crew, grew, flew, blew, etc.
6. Use the learning style you like best.
👂 If you are an auditory person: – say it aloud to yourself, sing it, turn it into a rap, quiz a friend.
👁 If you are a visual person practise write it; use different colours, look at the tall letters and short letters, draw pictures as clues, pretend your eyes are a camera and take a photo of it. Can you see a little word inside it?
✋ If you are a person who likes to learn by doing things, make huge letters in the air, walk up and down chanting it, do an action which links to the word, decide how many sounds are in the word and with the palm of your hand facing you, touch a finger as you say each sound.

7. For irregular words, think of associations/mnemonics to trigger your memory. Remember, the more ridiculous your rhyme, the easier it is to remember how to spell the word.

8. Talk about it and teach it to a friend or to a parent.

Let's learn to spell the word *'people'* using a technique with a very long name – 'Neuro-linguistic Programming' or NLP for short.

1. Ask your teacher to write *people* on a card in large lower case letters

2. Talk about the bit which make it hard to learn – You can't hear the o and you have to remember the /pul/ sound at the end is spelt *'ple'*

3. Now look up to the left and visualise (imagine you can see) the first letter *p* in the air or on a wall (you can choose a colour for it)

4. Now say *p* aloud

5. Now visualise the next letter *e* beside it

6. Start at the beginning and say the two letters aloud *pe*

7. Now say them backwards *ep*

   We do this to make sure you are visualising *pe*. You will find it hard to say it backwards if you are not visualising the letters

8. Then add the next letter, that silent one *o*. Pretend you are climbing through the circle it makes

9. Now say them from the beginning *peo* and backwards *oep*

10. Now add another *p*. Make sure it is the same size and colour as the first one

11. What do you have in the air now? Say *peop* and then backwards *poep*

12. Now add a tall *l*

13. What do you have? *peopl*   *lpoep*

14. Now for the last letter. Add another *e* in the same colour as the first *e*

15. What do you have? *people*. Backwards *elpoep*

16. Brilliant! Write it down

17. Now write a short sentence using it

18. Test yourself later in the day. If you think you have forgotten how to spell the word, look up to the left to help recall it. Then write another short sentence using the word.

19. Practise it every day for a week and keep your own spelling bank!

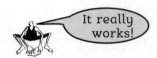

It really works!

abacus

abandon

  [abandoning abandoned]

abawt   about

abbey

abcent   absent

abdamen   abdomen

abdomen

abee   abbey

abel   able

ability   abilities

able

abnormal abnormally

abolish [abolishing abolished]

Aboriginal Aborigine

about

above

abowt   about

abracadabra

abrawd   abroad

abroad

absail   abseil

absant   absent

absawb   absorb

abseil [abseiling abseiled]

absence

absent absent-minded

abserd   absurd

absorb [absorbing absorbed]

absorbent

absurd absurdly

abuse [abusing abused]

abuv   above

abyus   abuse

accelerate

  [accelerating accelerated]

accelerator acceleration

accent

accept *[take]   except *[but]

  [accepting accepted]

acceptance

accident

accidental accidentally

accommodation

account [accounting accounted]

accountant

accross   across

accur   occur

accurate accurately

accuse [accusing accused]

ace

acelerate   accelerate

acent   accent

acept   accept

ache [aching ached] achy

acheive   achieve

achieve   achievement

   [achieving achieved]

acid   acid rain

Check out acc as well

acident   accident

acksel   axel *[jump]

                     axil *[leaf]

                     axle *[wheel]

acne

acorn

acownt   account

acre   acreage

acrobat   acrobatic

across

acselerate   accelerate

acsent   accent

acsept   accept

acshun   action

acsident   accident

act [acting acted]

actchely   actually

acter   actor

action   action-packed

active   actively

activetys   activities

activity   activities

actor   actress   actresses

actual   actually

acurate   accurate

acuse   accuse

acute   acutely

ad *[advert]   add *[sum]

Adam's apple

adapt [adapting adapted]

adaptable

add *[sum]   ad *[advert]

   [adding added]

addapt   adapt

addenoyds   adenoids

adder

addict [addicted] addiction

addition *[sum]   edition *[copy]

additional

additive

addoor   adore

address   addresses

   [addressing addressed]

ade   aid

adenoids

ader   adder

adhesive

adishun   addition

adjective

adjust   adjustable

2

admier   admire

admiral

admire [admiring admired]

admiration

admit [admitting admitted]

admyre   admire

adopt   adoption

adorable

adore [adoring adored]

adress   address

adult

advance

  [advancing advanced]

advantage

advencher   adventure

adventure   adventurous

adverb

advertise

  [advertising advertised]

advertisement

advice *[a tip]   advise *[suggest]

advise *[suggest]   advice *[a tip]

  [advising advised]

advurb   adverb

advurtise   advertise

ael   ale

aer   air

aerial

Check out air as well

aerodrome

aeroplane

aerosol

aery   airy

afar *[long]   affair *[event]

afect   affect *[alter]

             effect *[result]

affair

affect *[alter]   effect *[result]

affection   affectionate

affectionately

affekshun   affection

afford   affordable

affraede   afraid

afid   aphid

afloat

aford   afford

afraid

after

afternoon

afterwards

aftr   after

again

against

agane   again

3

age [ageing aged]

agectiv   adjective

agene   again

aggression

aggressive   aggressively

agile

ago

agony   agonies

agre   agree

agree [agreeing agreed]

agreeable

agreement

agreshun   aggression

agresiv   aggressive

agriculcher   agriculture

agriculture

aground

ahead

aid [aiding aided]

aim   aimless   aimlessly

air *[gas]   heir *[inherits]

air-conditioning

aircraft   aircraft carrier

airea   area

air   ~fare ~field ~lift

air   ~line ~mail ~raid

airial   aerial

airodrome   aerodrome

airoplane   aeroplane

airosol   aerosol

airport

airy

ais   ace

aisle *[passage]   isle *[island]

ajar

ajective   adjective

ajile   agile

ajust   adjust

ake   ache

Check out
ac as well

akselerayt   accelerate

akshun   action

aksident   accident

akt   act

aktiv   active

aktor   actor

Alah   Allah

alarm

alastik   elastic

album

alcohol   alcoholic

ale

alein   alien

alert [alerting alerted]

alevan   eleven
alfabet   alphabet
algae
algebra
algee   algae
alian   alien
alien
aligator   alligator
alight
alike
alite   alight
aliterashun alliteration
alive
aljebra   algebra
alkaline
alkohol   alcohol
all   all right
Allah
allarm   alarm
allergic   allergic reaction
allergy   allergies
allert   alert
alley *[path]   ally *[friend]
alligator
alliteration
allmost   almost
allot *[give]   a lot *[many]
allotment

allow [allowing allowed]
allowed *[may]   aloud *[talk]
alltho   although
alltogether   altogether
allurgic   allergic
allwase   always
allways   always
ally *[friend]   alley *[path]
almond
almost
aloan   alone
alone
along   alongside
a lot *[many]   allot *[give]
aloud *[talk]   allowed *[may]
alowed   allowed *[may]
             aloud *[talk]
alphabet   alphabetical
Alps   alpine
already
Alsation
also
altar *[church]
alter *[change] [altering altered]
alteration
alternative   alternatively
although
althow   although

altitude

altogether

alurt   alert

always

aly   ally *[friend]

         alley *[path]

alyke   alike

alyve   alive

am

amaze   amazement

Amazon

ambassador

ambel   amble

ambishun   ambition

ambition

ambitious

amble [ambling ambled]

amboosh   ambush

ambulance

ambush   ambushes

ame   aim

ameeba   amoeba

amen

amethyst

amfibian   amphibian

amfibious   amphibious

ammaze   amaze

ammunition

ammuse   amuse

amoeba

among   amongst

amount

amp

amphibian   amphibious

amputate   amputation

  [amputating amputated]

amung   among

amunishun   ammunition

amuse   amusement

amythist   amethyst

an

anagram

anceint   ancient

ancestor

anchor

ancient

ancor   anchor

and

anemone

aneversary   anniversary

anex   annexe

aney   any

angel *[God]   angle *[maths]

angelic   angelically

anger

angle *[maths]   angel *[God]

angler	
Anglo-Saxon	
angree	angry
angrily	
angry angrier angriest	
angur	anger
angziety	anxiety
animal	
animation	
animel	animal
aniseed	
aniversary	anniversary
anjel	angel
ankel	ankle
ankle	
ankor	anchor
ankshus	anxious
anmils	animals
annalise	analyse
annexe	
anniversary anniversaries	
annonymous	anonymous
annorak	anorak
annother	another
announce announcement	
annoy [annoying annoyed]	
annual annually	
anonymous anonymously	

anorak	
another	
anownce	announce
anoy	annoy
ansed	answered
anser	answer
ansestor	ancestor
anshent	ancient
answer [answering answered]	
ant *[insect]	aunt *[family]
Antarctic Antarctica	
antebyotic	antibiotic

Check out
anti as well

anteclimacks	anticlimax
anteek	antique
antehistameen	antihistamine
antelope	
antenna antennae	
antesoshall	antisocial
anthology anthologies	
antibiotic	
antic *[prank]	antique *[old]
anticeptic	antiseptic
anticlimax	
anticlockwise	
antihistamine	

antilope   antelope
antique *[old]   antic *[prank]
antiseptic
antisocial   antisocially
antler
antonym
anual   annual
anuther   another
anuver   another
anxiety   anxieties
anxious   anxiously
any   ~body ~how ~one
any   ~thing ~way ~where
aorta
aparant   apparent
apart
ape

Check out
app as well

apeal   appeal
apear   appear
apel   apple
apetight   appetite
aphid
aplie   apply
aplikashun   application
aplord   applaud

apologetic
apologise
  [apologising apologised]
apology   apologies
apon   upon
apostrofee   apostrophe
apostrophe
appalling   appallingly
apparatus
apparent   apparently
apparition
appart   apart
appeal   appealingly
appear [appearing appeared]
appearance
appendix   appendicitis
appetising
appetite
applaud   applause
  [applauding applauded]
apple
application
apply [applying applied]
appolagise   apologise
appreciate   appreciation
  [appreciating appreciated]
approach   approachable
  [approaching approached]

approval

approve [approving approved]

Aprel   April

apren   apron

apricot

April   April Fool's Day

aproch   approach

apron

apruve   approve

aquarium

Aquarius

Arab   Arabian   Arabic

arange   arrange

arc *[curve]   ark *[boat]

arcade

arch   arches

archaeology   archaeologist

archangel

archbishop

archer   archery

archiology   archaeology

architect   architecture

archor   archer

archway

Arctic   Arctic Circle

are *[we are]   our *[us]

area

areal   aerial

arena

aren't *[are not]   aunt *[family]

arest   arrest

argew   argue

argue

argument   argumentative

argyoumont   argument

arial   aerial

arithmetic

arival   arrival

arive   arrive

ark *[boat]   arc *[curve]

arkade   arcade

arkangel   archangel

arkiology   archaeology

arkitect   architect

Arktik   Arctic

arm   armchair

arma   armour

armada

armadillo

armed forces

armie   army

armond   almond

armour   armour-plated

army   armies

arnt   aren't *[are not]

     aunt *[family]

arodrome   aerodrome

arogant   arrogant

aroplane   aeroplane

arosol   aerosol

around

arow   arrow

arownd   around

arrange

   [arranging arranged]

arrangement

arrest [arresting arrested]

arrithmatic   arithmetic

arrival

arrive [arriving arrived]

arrogant   arrogantly

arrow   arrow-head

arsen   arson

arsenal

arsenic

arsk   ask

arsnick   arsenic

arson   arsonist

art

artcher   archer

arterie   artery

artery   arteries

arthritic   arthritis

artic   arctic

article

artificial   artificially

artifishall   artificial

artikal   article

artist   artistic

artrey   artery

as *[compare]   ass *[animal]

asassin   assassin

asassinate   assassinate

asc   ask

ascape   escape

ase   ace

asembly   assembly

asembul   assemble

ash   ashes   ashen

ashamed

Ashun   Asian

Asian

asist   assist

ask [asking asked]

asleep

asma   asthma

asortid   assorted

asparagus

ass *[animal]   as *[compare]

assassin   assassination

assassinate

   [assassinating assassinated]

assemble

[assembling assembled]

assembly   assemblies

assist [assisting assisted]

assistance   assistant

assorted   assortment

assume [assuming assumed]

Astec   Aztec

asterisk

asteroid

asthma   asthmatic

astonish   astonishment

astreisk   asterisk

astreoid   asteroid

astrologer

astronaut

astronomer   astronomy

astronort   astronaut

asume   assume

at

atach   attach

Check out
att as well

ate *[food]   eight *[number]

atempt   attempt

athlete   athletic   athletics

athority   authority

atic   attic

atishoo

atitude   attitude

Atlantic

atlas

atmosfere   atmosphere

atmosphere

atom   atom bomb

atomic   atomic energy

atract   attract

atractiv   attractive

attach [attaching attached]

attachment

attack [attacking attacked]

attempt [attempting attempted]

attend [attending attended]

attendance   attendant

attention

attentive   attentively

attic

attitude

attract [attracting attracted]

attraction   attractive

atyshoo   atishoo

aubergine

auburn

auction   auctioneer

audience

audishun — audition

audition

auditorium

auditory

auful — awful

August

aunt *[family]   ant *[insect]

  aren't *[are not]

au pair

aural   aurally

Aurgast — August

aut — out

author

authorisation   authority

authorise

  [authorising authorised]

autistic *[condition]

  artistic *[skill]

autism

autobiography

autograph

automatic   automatically

autopilot

autumn   autumnal

avacado — avocado

avacouatid — evacuated

available   availability

avalanche

avaleabul — available

avaperrat — evaporate

avapourate — evaporate

avary — aviary

avelanch — avalanche

avencherus — adventurous

avenew — avenue

aventure — adventure

avenue

average

averige — average

aviary   aviaries

aviashun — aviation

aviation   aviator

avlanch — avalanche

avocado

avoid [avoiding avoided]

avoyd — avoid

avrage — average

awair — aware

awake

award [awarding awarded]

aware   awareness

away

awayk — awake

awdiense — audience

awful   awfully

awght — ought

12

Awgust	August
awkward	awkwardly
awoke	awoken
awr	our
awt	ought
	out
awtumn	autumn
axe axes	
axel *[jump]	axle *[wheel]
axil *[leaf]	

axis axes	
axle *[wheel]	axel *[jump]
	axil *[leaf]
ayl	ale
aym	aim
ayt	eight *[number]
	ate *[food]
az	as

baa [baaing]

babble [babbling babbled]

babey   baby

babminton   badminton

baboon

babul   babble

baby   babyish

babysit   babysitter

  [babysitting babysat]

bac   back

bace   base *[bottom]

          bass *[music]

bacen   bacon

bach   batch

bachelor

back   ~ache ~stroke ~wards

backhand   backhanded

bacon

bacteria   bacterial

bad   badly   badness

bad   worse   worst

baddy   baddies

badge

badger

badminton

baffle [baffling baffled]

bag   bagpipes

bagage   baggage

bage   badge

bager   badger

baggage

baggy   baggier   baggiest

baige   beige

baik   bake

bail *[out, cricket]   bale *[bundle]

bailiff

bair   bare *[naked]

          bear *[carry, cub]

bairn

bais   base *[bottom]

bait [baited]

bak   back

bake [baking baked]

bakery

bakon   bacon

bakry   bakery

bakteria   bacteria

bal   ball *[kick]

balaclava

balad   ballad

balance

balcony

bald *[head]   bawled *[cried]

          bold *[strong]

bale *[bundle]   bail *[out, cricket]

balense   balance

balerina   ballerina

balkony   balcony

ball *[kick]   bawl *[cry]

ball

ballad

ballay   ballet

ballerina

ballet

balloon   balloonist

ballot

ballroom

balm

balmy *[mild]   barmy *[mad]

baloon   balloon

balot   ballot

balune   balloon

bamboo

bambu   bamboo

ban [banning banned]

banana

band *[group, stripe]

  banned *[stopped]

bandage

bandie   bandy

bandige   bandage

bandit

bandy   bandy-legged

baned   band *[group,
                        stripe]

        banned
                        *[stopped]

baner   banner

bang [banging banged]

bangle

banish   banishment

banister

banjo

bank

bankrupt   bankruptcy

bankwet   banquet

bannana   banana

banned *[stopped]

  band *[group, stripe]

banner

bannish   banish

bannister   banister

banquet

banter

baonnet   bayonet

baptise [baptising baptised]

baptism

bar *[pub]   bare *[naked]

bar *[stop]

barage   barrage

barax   barracks

barb   barbed

barbecue

barber

bare *[nude]   bear *[cub]

                        bear *[carry]

bare   barely

bare   ~foot ~headed ~legged

barekaid   barricade

barel   barrel

baren   baron *[noble]

                       barren *[dry]

bargain [bargaining bargained]

barge   barge-pole

bargin   bargain

baricade   barricade

barier   barrier

barister   barrister

barje   barge

bark

barley

barmaid   barman

barmy *[mad]   balmy *[mild]

barn

barnacle

barometer

baron *[noble]   barren *[dry]

barracks

barrel

barren *[dry]   baron *[noble]

barricade

barrier

barrister

barrow

barscit   basket

barter [bartering bartered]

barth   bath

bas   base *[bottom]

                      bass *[music]

bascet   basket

base *[bottom]   bass *[music]

basement

bash [bashing bashed]

bashful   bashfully

basic   basically

basin   basinful

basis   bases

bask [basking basked]

basket   basketball

basoon   bassoon

bass *[music]   base *[bottom]

bass-guitar   bass-guitarist

bassoon   bassoonist

baste [basting basted]

basyn   basin

bat   batsman

batalien   battalion

batcheler	bachelor
baten	baton
bater	batter
batery	battery
bath *[tub]	
bathe *[swim] [bathing bathed]	
batik	
batrie	battery
battalion	
battel	battle
batter [battering battered]	
battery	
battle	~field ~ground
batton	baton
battree	battery
batty battier battiest	
baul	ball *[sport, dance]
	bawl *[cry]
bawl *[cry]	ball *[kick]
bawt	bought
bay	
bayl	bale *[bundle]
	bail *[out, cricket]
bayliff	bailiff
bayonet	
bayt	bait
baything	bathing

bazaar
bcos — because
be *[being] — bee *[insect]
beach *[sea] — beech *[tree]
beacon
bead beady
beaf — beef
beak beaker
beam [beaming beamed]
bean *[food] — been *[was]
beap — beep
bear *[cub] — bare *[naked]
beard bearded
beast beastly
beat [beating beaten]
beautiful beautifully
beauty *[lovely] — booty *[loot]
beaver
became
because
beckon [beckoning beckoned]
become [becoming became]
becon — beckon
becos — because
becum — become
bed bed-linen
bedlam
Bedouin

17

bedroom   bedside

Bedwin   Bedouin

bee *[insect]   be *[being]

beech *[tree]   beach *[sea]

beed   bead

beef   beefy

beefburger

beehive

beek   beak

beem   beam

been *[was]   bean *[food]

beep [beeping beeped]

beer

beerd   beard

beest   beast

beestro   bistro

beetle

beever   beaver

befor   before

before   beforehand

befrend   befriend

befriend [befriending befriended]

beg [begging begged]

beggar

begin [beginning began]

beginner

behave [behaving behaved]

behaviour

behead [beheading beheaded]

behed   behead

behind

behvyer   behaviour

beige

being

bekame   became

bekause   because

bekon   beckon

bel   bell

belated   belatedly

belch [belching belched]

beleif   belief

beleive   believe

belfry   belfries

belief

believe   believable

   [believing believed]

belive   believe

bell   bell-ringing

bellow *[yell]   below *[under]

bellows

belly   bellyache

belly-button   belly-flop

belong [belonging belonged]

belongings

below *[under]   bellow *[yell]

belt

bench   benches

bend [bending bent]

beneath

beneeth   beneath

benefit

bent

berbul   burble

berd   bird

berden   burden

bereaved   bereavement

bereeved   bereaved

beret *[hat]   berry *[fruit]

                    bury *[cover]

Check out
bur as well

berger   burger

berglar   burglar

bergul   burgle

berial   burial

berly   burly

bern   burn

bernt   burnt

berry *[fruit]   beret *[hat]

                    bury *[cover]

berserk

berst   burst

berth *[bunk]   birth *[born]

bery   berry *[fruit]

                    bury *[cover]

beryed   buried

beseige   besiege

beside *[at the side]

besides *[apart from]

besiege [besieging besieged]

besotted

best

bet [betting betted bet]

betray [betraying betrayed]

better

between

beuteful   beautiful

beware

bewicht   bewitched

bewilder   bewilderment
  [bewildering bewildered]

bewitch [bewitching bewitched]

beyond

bhaji

bi   by *[near]

                    buy *[shop]

                    bye *[farewell]

biannual

bias   biased   biases

bib

Bible   biblical

biceps

bich — bitch

bicker [bickering bickered]

bicos — because

bicycle

bid [bidding bid]

Check out
be as well

bifour — before

big bigger biggest

bigan — began

biger — bigger

bigun — begun

bihave — behave

bihavior — behaviour

bihind — behind

bike

biker *[cyclist] — bicker *[row]

bikini

bil — bill

bilated — belated

bilberry bilberries

bild — billed *[invoiced]
— build *[construct]

bilding — building

bilevabul — believable

bilingual

bilion — billion

bill

billed *[pay] — build *[house]

billiards

billion billionaire

billy goat

biloved — beloved

bilow — below

bilt — built

bin *[box] — been *[was]

bind binder binding

bineath — beneath

binge

bingo

binoculars

biodegradable

biografer — biographer

biographer biography

biological

biologist biology

bipass — bypass

birch birches

bird bird-brained

birdbath birdseed

birden — burden

birdie

bird's-eye view

birger — burger

birgler	burglar
birgul	burgle
birnt	burnt
Biro™	
birth birthday	
biscit	biscuit
biscuit	
biseige	besiege
biseps	biceps
bishop	
biside	beside
biskit	biscuit
bison	
bistro	
bisycul	bicycle
bit	
bitch bitchy	
bite *[teeth]	byte *[data]
[biting bit bitten]	
bite-size bite-sized	
bitray	betray
bitter bitterly	
bitterness	
bitween	between
biware	beware
biwilder	bewilder
biy	buy
biyond	beyond

bizee	busy
bizness	business
blab [blabbing blabbed]	
black	~bird ~board
black	~currant ~out ~smith
Black Death	
blackberry blackberries	
bladder	
blade	
blader *[skater] bladder *[urine]	
blaid	blade
blaim	blame
blak	black
blame blameless	
blank blankly	
blanket	
blankit	blanket
blare [blaring blared]	
blarst	blast
blast blast-off	
blaze [blazing blazed]	
blazer	
bleach	
bleak bleakly bleakness	
bleat [bleating bleated]	
bleech	bleach
bleed [bleeding bled]	
bleek	bleak

bleep [bleeping bleeped]

bleet   bleat

blend

bler   blur

blert   blurt

bless [blessing blessed]

blew *[wind]   blue *[colour]

blind   blindly   blindness

blindfold   blind-man's-buff

blink [blinking blinked]

blip

bliss   blissful   blissfully

blister

Blitz [the]

blizzard

blo   blow

bloat [bloating bloated]

blob

bloch   blotch

blochy   blotchy

block [blocking blocked]

blockade

blockage

blod   blood

blog [blogging blogged]

bloke

blonde

blong   belong

blood   ~curdling ~hound

blood   ~shed ~shot ~stain

bloodthirsty

bloody

bloom [blooming bloomed]

blossom [blossoming blossomed]

blot [blotting blotted]

blotch   blotches   blotchy

blote   bloat

blouse

blow [blowing blew blown]

blubber   blubbery

blud   blood

blue *[colour]   blew *[wind]

bluebell   bluebottle

bluff [bluffing bluffed]

bluish

blume   bloom

blunder [blundering blundered]

blunt   bluntly   bluntness

blur [blurring blurred]

blurt [blurting blurted]

blush [blushing blushed]

bluwe   blue

blynd   blind

boa

boar *[pig]   bore *[dull]

board *[wood]   bored *[dull]

board [boarding boarded]

boast   boastful

boat   boating

bob   bobsleigh

bobble

bobul   bobble

boch   botch

body   bodies

bog   boggy

bogel   boggle

boggle [boggling boggled]

boggy

bogus

boil [boiling boiled]

boiler

boisterous   boisterously

bok   book

bolard   bollard

bold *[strong]   bald *[head]

                         bowled *[sport]

boldly

boler   bowler

bolinase   bolognaise

bollard

bolled   bald *[head]

                         bold *[strong]

                         bowled *[sport]

bolognaise [spaghetti]

bolshy

bolt [bolting bolted]

bom   bomb

bomb   bomb-disposal

bomb   ~shell ~site

bombard

  [bombarding bombarded]

bomber

bommer   bomber

bone

bonfire

Bonfire Night

bonkers

bonnet

bonus   bonuses

bony   bonier   boniest

booby   booby-prize

book   ~case ~shelf ~shop

bookay   bouquet

boom [booming boomed]

boomerang

boost [boosting boosted]

booster

boot

bootee *[shoe]   booty *[loot]

booteek   boutique

booth

booty *[loot]   bootee *[shoe]

borbul   bauble

border borderline

bordom   boredom

bordor   border

bore *[dull]   boar *[pig]

bored *[dull]   board *[wood]

boreding   boarding

boredom

born *[birth]

borne *[carried]

borrow [borrowing borrowed]

bort   bought

bosom

boss bossy

bost   boast

botanist botany

botch [botching botched]

bote   boat

botem   bottom

both

bother [bothering bothered]

botom   bottom

bottle bottle-feed

bottom bottomless

botul   bottle

botum   bottom

bough *[branch] bow *[bend]

bought *[buy] brought *[bring]

boukay   bouquet

boulder *[rock] bolder *[braver]

bounce [bouncing bounced]

bouncy bouncier

bound [bounding bounded]

boundary boundaries

bounse   bounce

bow *[bend]   bough *[branch]

bow *[arrow, knot]

bow [bowing bowed]

bowel *[tummy]

bowl *[dish]

bowl *[action] [bowling bowled]

bowler

bowndree   boundary

bownse   bounce

box boxes

boxer

Boxing Day

boy *[male]   buoy *[float]

boycott

boyfriend boyhood

boyish

boyl   boil

Boy Scout

boystrus   boisterous

bra bras

brace [bracing braced]

bracelet

bracken

bracket

brag [bragging bragged]

braid *[hair]   brayed *[ass]

braille

brain   brainwave

brainy   brainier   brainiest

brake *[slow]   break *[snap]

brake [braking braked]

braket   bracket

bramble

bran *[cereal]   brain *[mind]

branch   branches

brand   brand-new

brandish [brandishing brandished]

brane   brain

brar   bra

bras *[underwear] brass *[metal]

braselet   bracelet

brash

brass   brassy

brat   brattish   brattishly

braul   brawl

brave   braver   bravest

bravery

brawd   broad

brawl

brawt   brought

bray [braying brayed]

braynee   brainy

bread *[food]   breed *[type]

break *[snap]   brake *[slow]

break [breaking broke broken]

break   ~neck ~through

breakfast

breast   breastbone

breath   breathy

breathe [breathing breathed]

breathless   breathlessly

breathtaking

breaze   breeze

brecfst   breakfast

bred *[animal]   bread *[food]

                   breed *[type]

breed   breeder   breeding

breef   brief

breethe   breathe

breeze   breezy

breif   brief

brekfast   breakfast

brest   breast

breth   breath *[air]

                   breathe
                        *[in and out]

brethtaking   breathtaking

brew [brewing brewed]

brewed *[tea]   brood *[kids]

brewery   breweries

bribe [bribing bribed]

bribery

brick

bridal *[wedding] bridle *[horse]

bride   ~groom ~smaid

bridge

bridle *[horse]

  bridal *[wedding]

brief   briefest   briefly

brieze   breeze

brigade

brige   bridge

bright   brighter   brightest

brighten [brightening brightened]

brik   brick

brilliance

brilliant   brilliantly

brim

bring [bringing brought]

brisk   briskly

bristle   bristly

Britain *[place]   Briton *[person]

brite   bright

British

Briton *[person]   Britain *[place]

Britten   Britain

broad   broader   broadest

broaden [broadening broadened]

broadly

broak   broke

broccoli

broch   brooch

brocher   brochure

brochure

brocoli   broccoli

broke   broken

brokn   broken

bronse   bronze

brontosaurus

bronze   Bronze Age

brooch   brooches

brood *[kids]   brewed *[tea]

broody   broodier   broodiest

brook

broom   broomstick

broose   bruise

broot   brute

brord   broad

brort   brought

brother   brother-in-law

brought *[bring] bought *[buy]

brow

brown

brownie *[cake]

Brownie *[club]

browse [browsing browsed]

browser

brud   brood

brue   brew

bruise [bruising bruised]

brume   broom

brunch

brunette

brush   brushes

Brussels   brussels sprouts

brutal   brutally

brute   brutish

bruther   brother

brutle   brutal

brydal   bridal *[wedding]

             bridle *[horse]

bryde   bride

bubble [bubbling bubbled]

bubbly

bucher   butcher

buck [bucking bucked]

bucket [bucketing bucketed]

Buckingham Palace

buckle   buckles

bud [budding budded]

Buddha

Buddhism   Buddhist

buddy   buddies

budge [budging budged]

budgerigar   budgie

budget [budgeting budgeted]

Budha   Buddha

bufalo   buffalo

buffalo   buffaloes

buffay   buffet

buffet *[food]

buffet *[wind] [buffeted]

bug [bugging bugged]

bugel   bugle

bugerigar   budgerigar

buget   budget

buggy   buggies

bugle

build *[construct] billed *[invoiced]

building

built   built-up

bujet   budget

bul   bull

bulb   bulbous

bulee   bully

bulge [bulging bulged]

bulit   bullet

bulitin   bulletin

bulj   bulge

bulk   bulky

bull   bullock

bull   ~dog ~fight ~finch

bulldoze   bulldozer

  [bulldozing bulldozed]

bullet

bulletin

bullion

bully [bullying bullied]

bully   bullies

bulrush   bulrushes

buly   bully

bumble [bumbling bumbled]

bumblebee

bumerang   boomerang

bump [bumping bumped]

bumpy   bumpier   bumpiest

bun   bunfight

bunch   bunches

bundle [bundling bundled]

bung [bunging bunged]

bungalow

bungee

bungel   bungle

bungie   bungee

bungle [bungling bungled]

bunglo   bungalow

bunjie   bungee

bunk

bunker

bunny   bunnies

Bunsen burner

bunsh   bunch

buoy *[float]   boy *[male]

burble [burbling burbled]

burch   birch

burd   bird

burden [burdening burdened]

burgeld   burgled

burger

burglar

burglary   burglaries

burgle *[rob]   bugle *[horn]

burial

burly   burlier   burliest

burn [burning burned]

burnt

burp [burping burped]

burrow *[dig]   borrow *[loan]

bursar   bursary   bursaries

burst [bursting burst]

bursurk   berserk

burth   berth *[bunk]

                 birth *[born]

bury *[cover]   berry *[fruit]

bus   buses

busel   bustle

bush   bushes

bushy   bushier   bushiest

business   businesses

business   ~man ~woman

busker   busking

bussel   bustle

bustle [bustling]

busy   busier   busiest

but *[however]   butt *[hit]

buten   button

buter   butter

butie   beauty *[lovely]

               booty *[loot]

butiful   beautiful

butler

buton   button

butter   buttery

butter   ~cup ~fly ~scotch

buttock   buttocks

button   buttonhole

buty   beauty *[lovely]

             booty *[loot]

buy *[shop]   bye *[goodbye]

            by *[near]

buy [buying bought]

buzz [buzzes buzzing buzzed]

buzzard

bwuty   beauty

by *[near]   buy *[shop]

            bye *[goodbye]

byceps   biceps

Check out
bi as well

bycicul   bicycle

bye *[goodbye]   buy *[shop]

            by *[near]

byer   buyer

bynoculars   binoculars

bypass bypasses

   [bypassing bypassed]

byte *[data]   bite *[teeth]

Check out **K** as well

cab

cabale   cable

cabbage

cabin

cable

cackle [cackling cackled]

cactus   cacti

cadge [cadging cadged]

café *[snack]   coffee *[cup]

cage

caik   cake

caim   came

cair   care

caireful   careful

cake

calcium

calculate [calculating calculated]

calculation   calculator

calendar *[date] colander *[food]

calf *[baby cow] calves
                  calve *[give birth]

call [calling called]

calm   calmer   calmly

calorie   calories

calqulashun   calculation

calqulate   calculate

calqulator   calculator

calsium   calcium

calve *[give birth] carve *[cut]
  [calving calved]

camaflarge   camouflage

came

camel

camelion   chameleon

camera ~man

camouflage

camp   ~fire ~ground ~site

campaign
  [campaigning campaigned]

camra   camera

can *[able, tin]   cane *[stick]

canal

canary   canaries

cancel [cancelling cancelled]

cancellation

cancer *[illness]

Cancer *[zodiac]

candel   candle

candle   ~light ~lit ~stick

candy   ~floss

cane

canibal   cannibal

cannibal   cannibalism

cannon   cannonball

cannot

canoe [canoeing canoed]

cansel   cancel

canser   cancer *[illness]

           Cancer *[zodiac]

can't *[cannot]

canter [cantering cantered]

canue   canoe

canvas

canyon

cap *[hat, top]   cape *[cloak, land]

capable

capcher   capture

capillary   capillaries

capital

Capricorn

capshun   caption

capsize [capsizing capsized]

capsule

captain

capten   captain

capter   captor

caption

captive   captivity

capture

  [capturing captured]

car   carsick

caracter   character

caramel

carat *[gold]   carrot *[food]

caravan   caravanning

carbohydrate

carbon

carbord   cardboard

carcass   carcasses

card   cardboard

cardigan

cardinal

care   carefree

caree   carry

career *[job]   carrier *[carries]

careful   carefully

careless   carelessly

carelessness

caretaker   caretaking

cargo   cargoes

Caribbean

carier   career *[job]

           carrier *[carries]

carm   calm

carnation

carnival

carnivore   carnivorous

carol   carol-singing

carot   carat *[gold]

           carrot *[food]

carpenter   carpentry

carpet [carpeting carpeted]

carriage ~way

carrige   carriage

carrot *[food]   carat *[gold]

carry [carrying carried]

carsel   castle

cart *[transport] kart *[go-kart]

cart ~horse ~load ~wheel

carten   carton

carton *[box]

cartoon cartoonist

cartridge

cartune   cartoon

carve *[cut]   calve *[give birth]
  [carving carved]

carving

caryon   carrion

case [casing cased]

casel   castle

caset   cassette

cash *[money]   catch *[ball]

casheltee   casualty

cashew

cashier

cashmere

cashoe   cashew

casino

casserole   [casseroled]

cassette

cast castaway

caster *[sugar]   castor *[oil,
                         wheel]

castle

casual casually

casualty casualties

casum   chasm

cat

catacomb catacombs

catalogue catalogues

catapult [catapulting catapulted]

catar   catarrh

catarrh

catastrofee   catastrophe

catastrophe catastrophic

catch [catching caught]

category categories

catekoom   catacomb

catel   cattle

catelog   catalogue

catepolt   catapult

cater [catering catered]

caterpillar

cathedral

Catholic Catholicism

catkin

catnap [catnapping catnapped]

cattle

caturpillar   caterpillar

caught *[ball]   court *[law]

cauldron

cauliflower

cause [causing caused]

caushun   caution

caushus   cautious

caution [cautioning cautioned]

cautious   cautiously

cavalry

cave   caveman

cavity   cavities

cavurn   cavern

caw *[crow]   core *[centre]

                corps *[army]

cawling   calling

cawps   corpse

cayg   cage

caym   came

cease *[stop]   seize *[grab]

Check out **se** as well

ceaseless   ceaselessly

cedate   sedate

ceeje   siege

ceiling *[roof]   sealing

              *[fastening]

celebrate   celebration

  [celebrating celebrated]

celebrity   celebrities

celery

cell *[prison]   sell *[shop]

cellabration   celebration

cellar *[room]   seller *[sales

                      person]

cello   cellist

Celsius

Celt   Celtic

cement [cementing cemented]

cemetery   cemeteries

cene   scene *[theatre]

             seen *[eyes]

cenile   senile

census

cent *[money]   scent *[smell]

             sent *[away]

centaur

centenary

center   centre

centigrade

centimetre

centipede

centir   centre

central

centre [centring centred]

centry   sentry
centurion
century   centuries
cenyer   senior
cep   keep
ceramic
cerb   curb *[stop]
                kerb *[edge]
cercul   circle
cercus   circus
cereal *[grain]   serial *[sequence]
cerebral palsy
ceremonial
ceremony   ceremonies
cerf   serf *[slave]
                surf *[sea]
cerfew   curfew
cerial   cereal *[grain]
                serial *[sequence]
cerialise   serialise
cerkit   circuit
cername   surname
cerse   curse
cersor   cursor
certain *[sure]   curtain *[window]
certainty   certainties
certen   certain *[sure]
                curtain *[window]

certificate
certsy   curtsy
cerve   curve
cesspit
cew   cue *[signal]
                queue *[line]
chain [chaining chained]
chair
chaist   chased
chalet
chalinge   challenge
chalk   chalky
challenge [challenging challenged]
chamber
chameleon
champagne   campaign
     *[wine]   *[activity]
champion   championship
chance   chances   chancy
chandelier
chane   chain
change [changing changed]
changeable
chanj   change
channel   [channelling]
Channel [the English]
chanse   chance
chant [chanting chanted]

34

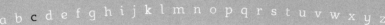
chaos   chaotic

chap

chapati

chapel   chaplain

chaplin   chaplain

chapter

chapul   chapel

character   characteristic

charade

charcoal

chare   chair

charge [charging charged]

chariot   charioteer

charitable

charity   charities

charm [charming charmed]

charnce   chance

charnt   chant

chart [charting charted]

charter flight

chase [chasing chased]

chasm   chasms

chat [chatting chatted]

chateau

chatter [chattering chattered]

chatty   chattier

chauffeur

chaw   chore

cheap *[money]   cheep *[bird]

cheap   cheaper   cheaply

cheat [cheating cheated]

check *[inspect]   cheque *[money]

  [checking checked]

checkmate

Cheddar cheese

cheef   chief

cheeften   chieftain

cheek

cheeky   cheekier   cheekiest

cheep *[bird]   cheap *[money]

cheepen   cheapen

cheer [cheering cheered]

cheerful   cheerfully

cheerfulness

cheese   ~burger ~cake

cheesy   cheesier   cheesiest

cheetah

chef *[cook]   chief *[boss]

cheir   chair

chello   cello

chemical   chemically

chemist   chemistry

cheque *[money] check *[inspect]

cherch   church

chere   chair

cheree   cherry

cherish [cherishes]

  [cherishing cherished]

chern   churn

cherry   cherries

cherub   cherubic

chess   chessboard

chest   chesty

chestnut

chew [chewing chewed]

chews *[food]   choose *[pick]

chewy   chewier   chewiest

chick

chicken   chickenpox

chickpea

chief   chiefs   chiefly

chieftain

chier   cheer

chiffon

chilblain

child   children   childish

chill [chilling chilled]

chilli *[food]   chillis

chilly *[cold]   chillier

chime [chiming chimed]

chimney   chimneys

chimp   chimpanzee

chin   chinless

china *[cup]   China *[place]

chinchilla

Chinese

chink

chip [chipping chipped]

chipmunk

chipolata

chirp [chirping chirped]

chirpy   chirpier   chirpiest

chisel [chiselling chiselled]

chivalry   chivalrous

chloride

chlorine

chlorophyll

chocerlit   chocolate

chocolate

chofer   chauffeur

choice

choir

choke [choking choked]

cholera

cholesterol

choose *[pick]   chews *[food]

  [choosing chose chosen]

choosy   choosier   choosiest

chop [chopping chopped]

chopsticks

choppy   choppier   choppiest

choral

chord *[music] cord *[rope]	churn [churning churned]
chore	churp chirp
chork chalk	chuse choose
chortle [chortling chortled]	chute *[slide] shoot *[target]
chorus choruses	chyna china
choys choice	cianide cyanide
Christ	cichin kitchen
christal crystal	ciclist cyclist
christen [christening christened]	ciclone cyclone
Christian Christianity	cicul cycle
Christmas	cider
chriy try	ciense science
chrome	cientific scientific
chromosome	cigar cigarette
chronic	cignet cygnet *[swan]
chronicle	signet *[ring]
chronological	cilindar cylinder
chrysalis chrysalises	cimbal cymbal *[music]
chrysanthemum	symbol *[sign]
chrystallise crystallise	cinder
chubby chubbier chubbiest	cinema
chuck [chucking chucked]	cinus sinus
chuckle [chuckling chuckled]	circit circuit
chue chew	circle
chug [chugging chugged]	circuit
chum chummy chummier	circular
chunk chunky chunkier	circulate circulation
church churches	[circulating circulated]

circumference

circumstance

circus   circuses

cissors   scissors

Check out
si as well

cissy   cissies

cist   cyst

citadel

cite *[quote]   sight *[seeing]

 [citing cited]   site *[place]

citee   city

citizen   citizenship

citrus

city   cities

civil   civilian

civilisation

civilise [civilising civilised]

clad

claim [claiming claimed]

clairvoyant

clam

clamber [clambering clambered]

clame   claim

clammy   clammier

clamp [clamping clamped]

clan

clang [clanging clanged]

clank [clanking clanked]

clap [clapping clapped]

clarinet   clarinettist

clarss   class

clash [clashes clashing clashed]

clasik   classic

clasp [clasping clasped]

class   classes

class   ~room ~work

classic   classical

clatter [clattering clattered]

clause *[part]   claws *[animal]

claustrophobia

claustrophobic

claw [clawing clawed]

claws *[animal]   clause *[part]

clay

clean [cleaning cleaned]

cleanliness   cleanly

cleanse [cleansing cleansed]

clear [clearing cleared]

clear   clearly

cleen   clean

cleer   clear

cleeshay   cliché

clementine

clench [clenching clenched]

clense	cleanse
clergy	
clever cleverer cleverest	
cleverly cleverness	
clew	clue
cliché	
client	
cliff cliffhanger	
clik	click
clim	climb
climate climatic	
climax climaxes	
climb [climbing climbed]	
climed	climbed
climing	climbing
cling [clinging clung]	
clinic	
clink [clinking clinked]	
clip [clipping clipped]	
cloak cloakroom	
clobber [clobbering clobbered]	
clock clockwork	
clockwatch [clockwatches]	
clog [clogged]	
cloke	cloak
clone	
clorafill	chlorophyll
clore	claw

cloride	chloride
clorinate	chlorinate
clorine	chlorine
clorofill	chlorophyll
clors	clause *[part]
	claws *[animal]
clorstrofobia	claustrophobia
close [closing closed]	
close closer closest	
closely closeness	
closet	
clot [clotting clotted]	
cloth *[material]	
clothe *[put clothes on]	
clothes clothing	
cloud cloudless	
cloudy cloudier cloudiest	
clout [clouting clouted]	
clove	
clover	
clowd	cloud
clown clownish	
clowt	clout
club [clubbing clubbed]	
cluch	clutch
cluck [clucking clucked]	
clue clueless	
clump [clumping clumped]	

clumpy   clumpier   clumpiest

clumsy   clumsier   clumsiest

clunk [clunking clunked]

clurgy   clergy

cluster [clustering clustered]

clutch   clutches

  [clutching clutched]

clutter [cluttering cluttered]

clyent   client

clyme   climb

coach   coaches

  [coaching coached]

coal   coalmine

coarse   coarsely

coast   ~guard ~line

coastal

coat

cobble   cobblestone

  [cobbling cobbled]

cobra

cobweb

Coca Cola™

coch   coach

cock   cock-a-doodle-doo

cockatoo

cockerel

cockney

cockpit

cockroach   cockroaches

cocky   cockier   cockiest

cocoa

coco   cocoa

coconut

cocoon [cocooning cocooned]

cocune   cocoon

cod

code

coed   could

coff   cough

coffee *[cup]   café *[snack]

coffin

cohort

coil [coiling coiled]

coin [coining coined]

coincidence

cokatoo   cockatoo

cola *[drink]   collar *[neck]

colander *[food] calendar *[time]

colaps   collapse

cold   colder   coldest

coldly   coldness

cole   coal

coleeg   colleague

coler   collar *[neck]

                   colour *[red]

colera   cholera

colerbone	collarbone
colerful	colourful
coleslaw	
colesterol	cholesterol
colide	collide
colige	college
collage	
collapse	collapsible
[collapsing collapsed]	
collar	collarbone
collarj	collage
colleague	
collecshun	collection
collect	collector
[collecting collected]	
collection	
college	
collide [colliding collided]	
colliflower	cauliflower
collision	
colloquial	
collum	column
colon	
colonel *[army]	kernel *[seed]
colony	colonies
coloqueal	colloquial
colour	colourless
colourful	colourfully

column	
coma *[sleep]	comma *[text]
comando	commando
comb	
combat	
combine	combination
[combining combined]	
come [coming came]	
comedian comedy	comedies
comeing	coming
comemorate	commemorate
comen	common
comense	commence
coment	comment
comentry	commentary
comershal	commercial
comet *[sky]	commit *[to do]
comforball	comfortable
comfort [comforting comforted]	
comfortable	comfortably
comfy	
comic	comical
comidian	comedian
coming	
comit	comet *[sky]
	commit *[to do]
comitee	committee
comma *[text]	coma *[sleep]

41

command   commander
  [commanding commanded]
commando
commemorate
commence
  [commencing commenced]
comment   commentator
  [commenting commented]
commentary   commentaries
commer   comma
commercial   commercially
commic   comic
commit *[to do]   comet *[sky]
commit   commitment
  [committing committed]
committee
common   commonly
Commonwealth Games
commotion
communicate
  [communicating communicated]
communication
communism   communist
community   communities
commute   commuter
  [commuting commuted]
comon   common
comoshun   commotion

compact
compair   compare
companion
company   companies
companyon   companion
compare   comparison
  [comparing compared]
compartment
compashun   compassion
compass   compasses
compassion   compassionate
compeet   compete
compensate   compensation
  [compensating compensated]
compete   competitor
  [competing competed]
competent   competently
competition   competitive
compitishun   competition
complain   complaint
  [complaining complained]
complane   complain
compleks   complex
complekshun   complexion
complete   completely
  [completing completed]
complex
complexion

complicate   complication
  [complicating complicated]
compliment   complimentary
compose [composing composed]
compost
compound
comprehend
  [comprehending comprehended]
comprehension
  comprehensive
comprihenshun comprehension
compulsion   compulsive
compulsory
computer
comunicate   communicate
comunism   communism
comunitee   community
comute   commute
con [conning conned]
concave
conceal [concealing concealed]
conceit   [conceited]
concensus   consensus
concentrate   concentration
  [concentrating concentrated]
concepshun   conception
concept
conception

concequense   consequence
concern [concerning concerned]
concert
concienshus   conscientious
concious   conscious
concise   concisely
concist   consist
concistency   consistency
conclewd   conclude
conclude   conclusion
  [concluding concluded]
concoct   concoction
  [concocting concocted]
concrete
concussed   concussion
condem   condemn
condemn   condemnation
  [condemning condemned]
condense   condensation
  [condensing condensed]
condishun   condition
condition   conditional
conditioner
conduct   conductor
  [conducting conducted]
cone
conference
conferm   confirm

confess   confession
  [confessing confessed]
confest   confessed
confetti
confide   confidence
  [confiding confided]
confident   confidently
confidential   confidentially
confine   [confined]
confirm   confirmation
  [confirming confirmed]
confiscate   confiscation
  [confiscating confiscated]
conflict
confrence   conference
confront   confrontation
  [confronting confronted]
confuse   confusion
  [confusing confused]
confyde   confide
congrachulate   congratulate
congratulate
  [congratulating congratulated]
congratulations
conical
conifer   coniferous
conjer   conjure
conjunction

conjure   conjuror
  [conjuring conjured]
conkave   concave
conker *[nut]   conquer *[win]
conkrete   concrete
conkussed   concussed
conkwest   conquest
connect   connection
  [connecting connected]
conquer *[win]   conker *[nut]
conqueror   conquest
conscience
conscientious
conscientiously
conscious   consciously
conseat   conceit
consecutive   consecutively
conseel   conceal
conseive   conceive
consensus
consent [consenting consented]
consentrashun   concentration
consentrate   concentrate
consept   concept
consequence
consern   concern
consert   concert
conservation

conservative

conservatory

conserve [conserving conserved]

conshense   conscience

conshienshus   conscientious

conshus   conscious

consider   considerable

  [considering considered]

considerate   consideration

consise   concise

consist [consisting consisted]

consistent   consistently

consolation prize

console [consoling consoled]

consonant

conspiracy   conspiracies

constable

constant

constellation

constipated   constipation

construcshun   construction

construct   construction

  [constructing constructed]

constructive   constructively

consult   consultant

  [consulting consulted]

consume   consumer

  [consuming consumed]

consurlashun   consolation

consurvashun   conservation

consurvativ   conservative

consurvatory   conservatory

consyoum   consume

contact [contacting contacted]

contagious

contain   container

  [containing contained]

contajus   contagious

contaminate   contamination

  [contaminating contaminated]

contane   contain

contemplate   contemplation

  [contemplating contemplated]

contemporary

  contemporaries

contempt

content   contentment

contest   contestant

  [contesting contested]

context

continent *[land mass]

Continent *[the]

continual   continually

continuation

continue   continuity

  [continuing continued]

continuous   continuously

contour

contract   contractor

  [contracting contracted]

contradict   contradiction

  [contradicting contradicted]

contraption

contrary

contrast [contrasting contrasted]

contredict   contradict

contrery   contrary

contribute   contributor

  [contributing contributed]

contribution

control   controllable

  [controlling controlled]

controversy   controversial

convay   convey

convayer belt   conveyor belt

convecshun   convection

convection   convector

conveks   convex

convenient   conveniently

convent

conversation

conversion

convert   convertible

  [converting converted]

convex

convey [conveying conveyed]

conveyor belt

convict   conviction

  [convicting convicted]

convince [convincing convinced]

convinient   convenient

convinse   convince

convoy

convulse [convulsed]

convulsion

convursashun   conversation

convurshun   conversion

convurt   convert

cood   could

cook   cooker

  [cooking cooked]

cookery

cool   cooler   coolest

coolly

co-operate   co-operation

  [co-operating co-operated]

co-operative

co-operatively

co-ordinashun   co-ordination

co-ordinate   co-ordinator

  [co-ordinating co-ordinated]

co-ordination

cop *[get] [copping copped]

cope *[deal with] [coping coped]

copie   copy

co-pilot

copper

copy   copies [copying copied]

coral *[sea]   choral *[sing]

Coran   Koran

cord *[rope]   chord *[music]

corduroy

core *[centre]   caw *[crow]

          corps *[army]

corel   choral *[sing]

          coral *[sea]

corespond   correspond

corght   caught *[ball]

          court *[law]

corige   courage

corjet   courgette

cork   corkscrew

corldron   cauldron

corled   called

cormorant

corn   corn-on-the-cob

corner

cornet

corny

corode   corrode

corporal

corprel   corporal

corps *[army]

corpse *[body]

corral *[pen]   coral *[sea]

correct   correction

   [correcting corrected]

correspond   correspondence

   [corresponding corresponded]

corridor

corroad   corrode

corrode [corroding corroded]

corrugated iron

cors   cause *[reason]

          course *[order,

                path]

corse   cause *[reason]

          coarse *[rough]

          course *[order,

                path]

corshun   caution

cort   caught *[ball]

          court *[law]

cortier   courtier

cortmarshall   court-martial

coschume   costume

cosee   cosy

cosmetic

cosmonaut

cost *[value]   coast *[sea]

cost   costly

coste   coast

costume

cosy   cosier   cosiest

cot *[bed]   coat *[clothing]

coton   cotton

cottage

cotton

couch   couches

cough

could   couldn't [could not]

counsellor

count   counter

  [counting counted]

countess

country   countries

county   counties

couple

couplet

courage

courageous   courageously

courd   cord *[rope]

                   chord *[music]

courgette

courier

course *[meal]   coarse *[rough]

coursework

court *[law]   caught *[ball]

courteous   courteously

courtesy *[polite] curtsy *[bow]

court-martial

cousin

cove

cover [covering covered]

cow   ~boy ~girl ~slip

coward

cowardly   cowardice

cowch   couch

cownsel   council

                   *[assembly]

counsel *[advise]

  [counselling counselled]

cownseller   counsellor

                   *[adviser]

cownt   count

coyn   coin

cozmetic   cosmetic

cozmic   cosmic

cozmonort   cosmonaut

crab   crabby

crack [cracking cracked]

crackle [crackling crackled]

cradle [cradling cradled]

craft   craftsman

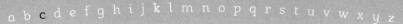
crafty   craftier   craftiest
crag   craggy
craip   crepe *[paper]
                         crêpe *[pancake]
craizee   crazy
crak   crack
crakul   crackle
cram [cramming crammed]
cramp [cramping cramped]
cranberry   cranberries
crane [craning craned]
crank [cranking cranked]
cranky   crankier   crankiest
crash *[accident]   crashes
                    crush *[squash]
crash [crashes crashing crashed]
crate *[box]
crater *[large hole]
crawl [crawling crawled]
crayon
craze   crazy   crazier
creacher   creature
creak   creaky
cream   creamy
creap   creep
crease [creasing creased]
create   creator   creation
  [creating created]

creative   creatively
creativity
creature
crèche
crecher   creature
credit [credited]
creem   cream
creep   creeper   creepy
  [creeping crept]
creese   crease
cremation   crematorium
crepe *[paper]
crêpe *[pancake]
crepey   creepy
crept
crescent
cress
cressent   crescent
crevasse *[ice]
crevice *[crack]
crew
criashun   creation
criate   create
criativ   creative
crib
cricket   cricketer
crie   cry
cried

crikit   cricket

crime

criminal

crimson

cringe [cringing cringed]

crinj   cringe

crinkle   crinkly

cript   crypt

crisis   crises

crisp   crispy   crispier

crissen   christen

Crist   Christ

cristal   crystal

criteria

critic   critical   critically

criticise   criticism

   [criticising criticised]

critisize   criticise

croak   croaky   croakier

   [croaking croaked]

crock   crockery

crocodile

crocus   crocuses

crokay   croquet

croke   croak

crokodile   crocodile

crokus   crocus

crome   chrome

crook   crooked

crop [cropping cropped]

croquet

crorl   crawl

cross   crosser   crossly

cross   ~roads ~word

crouch [crouching crouched]

croud   crowd

crow [crowing crowed]

crowch   crouch

crowd *[people]

crowed *[cockerel]

crowkay   croquet

crown [crowning crowned]

cruch   crutch

crucified   crucifix

crude   crudely

crue   crew

cruel   crueller

cruelly   cruelty

cruise *[trip]   crews *[teams]

crumb   crumbly

crumble *[break]

   [crumbling crumbled]

crumple *[crease] [crumpled]

crunch   crunchy   crunchier

   [crunching crunched]

crusade   crusader

crush [crushing crushed]

crust   crusty

crutch   crutches

cry   cries

cry [cries crying cried]

crysalis   chrysalis

crysanthemum
                chrysanthemum

crystal

cryticysum   criticism

cub

cube   cuboid

cubicle

cubord   cupboard

cuckoo

cucumber

cud

cuddle   cuddly [cuddling cuddled]

cue *[signal]   queue *[line]

cuff   cufflink

culcher   culture

cule   cool

cull [culling culled]

culla   colour

culprit

cultivate   cultivator
    [cultivating cultivated]

cultivation

culture   cultural

cum   come

cumfertabul   comfortable

cumfort   comfort

cumfy   comfy

cumpanee   company

cumpass   compass

cunning   cunningly

cuntree   country

cup   cupful   cuppa

cupboard

Cupid

cuple   couple

curb *[stop]   kerb *[edge]

cure [curing cured]

curensy   currency

curent   currant *[fruit]
                current *[flow,
                        now]

curfew

curier   courier

curiosity

curious   curiously

curl [curling curled]

curly   curlier

currage   courage

currant *[fruit]   current *[flow,
                        now]

currency   currencies

current *[flow,   currant *[fruit]
        now]

current   currently

curriculum

curry   curries

curse [cursing cursed]

cursive

cursor

curtain *[net]   certain *[sure]

curtificate   certificate

curtsy *[bow]   courtesy
                          *[polite]

curve [curving curved]

cury   curry

cushion

cusin   cousin

custard

custody

custom   customer

cut *[with a knife]   cutter
  [cutting cut]

cute *[sweet] cuter   cutest

cutlery

cuver   cover

cyanide

cyberspace

cycle [cycling cycled]

cyclist

cyclone   cyclonic

cygnet *[swan]   signet *[ring]

cylinder   cylindrical

cymbal *[music] symbol *[sign]

cymbolic   symbolic

cynonim   synonym

cyringe   syringe

cyrup   syrup

cystem   system

cyte   sight

czar   czarina

Check out
sy as well

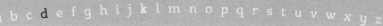
D-Day

dab [dabbing dabbed]

dabble [dabbling dabbled]

dabel   dabble

Dachshund

dad daddy daddies

daffodil

daft dafter daftest

dagger

daily

dair   dare

dairy *[milk]   diary *[book]

daisy daisies

Dalmashun   Dalmatian

Dalmatian

dam *[water]   damn *[curse]

damage [damaging damaged]

dame

damige   damage

damn *[curse]   dam *[water]
  [damning damned]

damp dampness

dampen [dampening dampened]

damson

dance [dancing danced]

dandelion

dandruff

dandylion   dandelion

danger dangerous

dangerously

dangle [dangling dangled]

dangros   dangerous

danjer   danger

dank

dans   dance

dapple [dappling dappled]

dare [daring dared]

darey   dairy

dark darkly darkness

darken [darkening darkened]

darling

darn [darning darned]

dart [darting darted]

dash dashes [dashing dashed]

data database

date [dating dated]

daughter

daun   dawn

dauter   daughter

dawdle dawdler
  [dawdling dawdled]

dawn [dawning dawned]

daxhound   Dachshund

day ~break ~dream ~light

dayity   deity

dayly   daily

days *[dates]   daze *[stun]

dayt   date

daze *[stun]   days *[dates]

dazzle [dazzling dazzled]

dead *[not alive]   deed *[action]

deaden [deadening deadened]

deadly   deadlier

deaf   deafness

deafen [deafening deafened]

deafeningly

deal [dealing dealt]

dealer   dealership

dealt

dear *[loved]   deer *[animal]

dearest   dearly

death   deathly

debait   debate

debatable

debate [debating debated]

debt   debtor

decade   decayed
    *[10 years]   *[rotted]

decarate   decorate

decay [decaying decayed]

deceit   deceitful

deceitfully   deceitfulness

deceive [deceiving deceived]

December

decent *[good]   descent *[down]

decently

deception

deceptive   deceptively

decibel

decide [deciding decided]

decidedly

deciduous

decimal

decipher [deciphering deciphered]

decision

deck [decking decked]

declaration

declare [declaring declared]

decline [declining declined]

decode [decoding decoded]

decomposed

decorate   decorator
    [decorating decorated]

decoration

decorative   decoratively

decoy

decrativ   decorative

decrease   decreasingly
    [decreasing decreased]

decree *[law]   degree *[uni]

ded   dead *[not alive]

                deed *[action]

dedicate   dedication

  [dedicating dedicated]

deduct   deduction

  [deducting deducted]

deed *[action]   dead *[not alive]

deel   deal

deep   deeply

deepen [deepening deepened]

deepfreeze   deep-frozen

deer *[animal]   dear *[loved]

deezel   diesel

def   deaf

defeat [defeating deafeated]

defect

defence   defenceless

defend   defendant

  [defending defended]

defens   defence

defensive   defensively

deffen   deafen

defiant   defiantly

define [defining defined]

definetly   definitely

definishun   definition

definite   definitely

definition

deform [deformed]

deformity   deformities

defrost [defrosting defrosted]

defuse [defusing defused]

defy [defies defying defied]

degree *[uni]   decree *[law]

dehydrate [dehydrated]

de-ice [de-icing de-iced]

deity   deities

deject [dejected]   dejection

dek   deck

dekorate   decorate

delay [delaying delayed]

delete   deletion [deleting deleted]

deliberate   deliberately

  [deliberating deliberated]

delicacy   delicacies

delicate   delicately

delicatessen

delicious   deliciously

delight [delighting delighted]

delightful   delightfully

delinquent   delinquency

delishus   delicious

deliver   deliverer

  [delivering delivered]

delivery   deliveries

delt   dealt

deluge [deluged]

demand [demanding demanded]

demented   dementia

demerara

demist [demisting demisted]

demo

democratic   democratically

demolish [demolishes]

 [demolishing demolished]

demolition

demon   demonic

demonstrate   demonstration

 [demonstrating demonstrated]

demoralise

 [demoralising demoralised]

den

dencher   denture

denial

denim

denomination   denominator

dense *[thick]   dents *[dips]

density

dent [denting dented]

dental

dentist   denture

deny [denies denying denied]

denyal   denial

deodorant

depart   departure

 [departing departed]

department

depend   dependable

 [depending depended]

dependence   dependent

depict [depicting depicted]

depo   depot

deport [deporting deported]

deportation

deposit

depot

depress   depression

 [depressing depressed]

deprive   deprivation

 [depriving deprived]

depth

deputy

derail [derailing derailed]

derelict

dert   dirt

descant

descend   descendant

 [descending descended]

descent *[down]   decent *[good]

descrete   discreet

describe [describing described]

description   descriptive

deseet   deceit

Desember   December

desent	decent
desert *[sand]	dessert *[food]
desert *[leave]	desertion
deserve	deservedly
[deserving deserved]	
desibell	decibel
deside	decide
desifer	decipher
design	designer
[designing designed]	
desimal	decimal
desirable	
desire [desiring desired]	
desk	
despair	despairingly
[despairing despaired]	
desperashun	desperation
desperate	desperately
desperation	
despise [despising despised]	
despite	
deposit [depositing deposited]	
despute	dispute
dessend	descend
dessent	decent *[good]
	descent *[down]
dessert *[food]	desert *[sand]
	desert *[leave]

destination
destiny [destined]
destroy destroyer
  [destroying destroyed]
destruction
destructive destructively
det   debt
detail [detailing detailed]
detain [detaining detained]
detect [detecting detected]
detectable detection
detector detective
detention
deter deterrant
  [deterring deterred]
detergent
deteriate   deteriorate
deteriorate deterioration
  [deteriorating deteriorated]
determination
determine determined
detest detestable
  [detesting detested]
deth   death
detonate detonator
  [detonating detonated]
detour
deuce

57

devastate   devastation
  [devastating devastated]
develop   development
  [developing developed]
device *[thing]   devise *[invent]
devide   divide
devil
devious   deviously
devise *[invent]   device *[thing]
devorse   divorce
devoshun   devotion
devote [devoting devoted]
devotion
devour [devouring devoured]
devout   devoutly
devyce   device *[thing]
                       devise *[invent]
dew *[drops]   Jew *[religion]
                       due *[owing]
dewet   duet
dewy
diabetes   diabetic
diafram   diaphragm
diagnose [diagnosed]
diagnosis   diagnoses
diagonal   diagonally
diagram
dial [dialling dialled]

dialect
dialogue
diameter
diamond
diaphragm
diar   dire *[bad]
                     dear *[loved]
                     deer *[animal]
diarrhoea
diarria   diarrhoea
diary *[book]   dairy *[milk]
dibate   debate

Check out
di as well

dice
diceive   deceive
dicree   decree
dicshunry   dictionary
dictate   dictation
  [dictating dictated]
dictator   dictatorship
dictionary   dictionaries
did *[do]   died *[die]
dide   died
dident   didn't
didn't [did not]
diduct   deduct

58

die *[death]*   dye *[colour]*
 [dies dying died]

died *[death]*   did *[do]*
                    dyed *[colour]*

diesel

diet [dieting dieted]

difend   defend

differ [differing differed]

different   differently

difficult

difficulty   difficulties

difrens   difference

difrent   different

dify   defy

dig [digging dug]

digest [digesting digested]

digestion   digestive

digit   digital   digitally

dignify   dignified

dignity

digraph

digree   degree

diing   dyeing *[colour]*
                    dying *[about to
                              die]*

dijestshun   digestion

dijital   digital

dikshunrey   dictionary

diktater   dictator

dilapidated

dilay   delay

dilect   dialect

dilemma

dilete   delete

diling   dialling

dilinquent   delinquent

dilishus   delicious

dilute [diluting diluted]

dimand   demand

dimensha   dementia

dimension

dimentid   demented

diminish [diminishing diminished]

dimple [dimpled]

din

dinasty   dynasty

dinatime   dinner time

dine [dining dined]

dinghy *[boat]*   dingy *[dull]*

dingo   dingoes

dingy *[dull]*   dinghy *[boat]*

dinial   denial

dinner

dinosaur

diodorant   deodorant

dioxide

dip [dipping dipped]

dipacher   departure

dipart   depart

diploma

diplomacy

diplomat   diplomatic

diposzit   deposit

dire

direct [directing directed]

direction   directly

directness   director

directory   directories

dirt   dirty   dirtier

disability   disabilities

disable   disabled

disadvantage

disagree   disagreeable

disagreed   disagreement

disappear   disappearance
  [disappearing disappeared]

disappoint   disappointment
  [disappointing disappointed]

disapproval

disapprove
  [disapproving disapproved]

disarm [disarming disarmed]

disaster   disastrous

disastrously

disbelief

disc *[circle,   disk *[computer]
      music]

discend   descend

discharge [discharging discharged]

disciple

discipline   disciplined

disco   discotheque

discomfort

disconnect [disconnected]

discontented

discotech   discotheque

discount [discounted]

discourage   discouragement
  [discouraging discouraged]

discover   discovery
  [discovering discovered]

discreet   discreetly

discribe   describe

discriminate   discrimination
  [discriminating discriminated]

discripshun   description

discurige   discourage

discus *[throw]

discuss *[talk]   discussion
  [discussing discussed]

disease   diseased

disect   dissect

60

disembark
[disembarking disembarked]

disepshun   deception

diseptiv   deceptive

disert   desert *[leave]

    dessert *[food]

diserve   deserve

diseve   deceive

disgrace [disgracing disgraced]

disgraceful   disgracefully

disgruntled

disguise [disguised]

disgust [disgusting disgusted]

dish   dishes

dishevelled

dishonest   dishonestly

dishonesty

diside   decide

disiduus   deciduous

disillusion [disillusioned]

disine   design

disinfect   disinfectant
[disinfecting disinfected]

disintegrate   disintegration
[disintegrating disintegrated]

disirabul   desirable

disire   desire

disjointed

disk *[computer]   disc *[circle, music]

diskomfort   discomfort

dislexsia   dyslexia

dislike [disliked]

dislodge [dislodged]

disloyal

dismal   dismally

dismiss   dismissal
[dismissing dismissed]

disobedience   disobedient

disobey [disobeying disobeyed]

disorder   disorderly

disorganise [disorganised]

disorganisation

disorientated

disown [disowning disowned]

dispair   despair

dispatch   dispatches
[dispatching dispatched]

disperse [dispersed]

dispise   despise

dispite   despite

display [displaying displayed]

displeased

dispose   [disposing disposed]

disposable   disposal

dispraxia   dyspraxia

disprove *[deny] disapprove
*[bad]

dispute [disputing disputed]

disqualification

disqualify disqualifies
[disqualifying disqualified]

disregard [disregarded]

disrespectful disrespectfully

disrupt disruption
[disrupting disrupted]

disruptive disruptively

dissapear disappear

dissapoint disappoint

disscurrage discourage

dissect dissection
[dissecting dissected]

dissendent descendant

dissert desert *[leave]
dessert *[food]

dissiplin discipline

dissolve [dissolving dissolved]

dissproov disprove

distance

distant distantly

distilled distillery

distinct distinctly

distinction

distinctive distinctively

distinguish [distinguishes]
[distinguishing distinguished]

distort distortion
[distorting distorted]

distract distraction
[distracting distracted]

distress [distresses]
[distressing distressed]

distribute [distributing distributed]

distribution distributor

district

distroy destroy

distructiv destructive

distrust distrustful
[distrusting distrusted]

disturb disturbance
[disturbing disturbed]

disused

disyfer decipher

ditch ditches [ditching ditched]

ditectiv detective

ditenshun detention

diter deter

ditermin determine

ditest detest

dither [dithering dithered]

dive [diving dived]

divelop develop

diversion

divert [diverting diverted]

divice   device

divide [dividing divided]

divine   divinely

divisible

division   divisor

divorce [divorcing divorced]

divurtid   diverted

dizease   disease

dizzy   dizzier   dizziest

dlishus   delicious

do *[act]   doe *[deer]

do [does doing did]

dock [docking docked]

doctor

document   documentary
    [documenting documented]

doddery

dodge [dodging dodged]

dodgy   dodgier

dodgem

doe *[deer]   dough *[bread]

does   doesn't [does not]

dog   dogged   doggy

doj   dodge

dojem   dodgem

dokter   doctor

dole [doling doled]

dolfin   dolphin

doll   dolly   dollies

dollar

dollop

dolphin

dome *[shape]   doom *[gloom]

Domesday Book

domestic

dominance   dominant

dominate   domination
    [dominating dominated]

domino   dominoes

donate   donation
    [donating donated]

done

donkey   donkeys

donor

don't [do not]

doodle [doodling doodled]

doom [doomed]

Doomsday   Domesday *[Book]

door   doorknob

dooy   do

dope   dopey

dordul   dawdle

dormitory   dormitories

dormouse   dormice

dorn — dawn

dorter — daughter

dosage

dose *[medicine]   does *[do]

doze *[nap]

dotty   dottier

double [doubling doubled]

doubly

doubt [doubting doubted]

doubtful   doubtless

dough *[bread]   doe *[deer]

dove   dovecote

dow — do

dowdy   dowdier

down [downing downed]

downstairs   downstream

downwards   downwind

downy

dowtful — doubtful

doze   dozy   dozier

[dozing dozed]

dozen

drag [dragging dragged]

draggen — dragon

dragon   dragonfly

drain [draining drained]

drainage   drainpipe

drake

drama   dramatic

dramatically

dramatise

[dramatising dramatised]

drank

drastic   drastically

draught   draughty

draw *[pull, art]

[drawing drew]

drawer *[box]

drawn   drawn-out

dread [dreading dreaded]

dreadful   dreadfully

dream [dreaming dreamt]

dreamy   dreamier

dreary   drearier

dred — dread

dredge [dredging dredged]

dreem — dream

dregs

drej — dredge

dreme — dream

drench [drenching drenched]

dresarje — dressage

dress [dressing dressed]

dress   dresses   dressmaker

dressage

drew

drey

dribble [dribbling dribbled]

dribiling · dribbling

dride · dried

drie · dry

dried

drier *[less wet] · dryer *[machine]

drift [drifting drifted]

drill [drilling drilled]

drink [drinking drank drunk]

drip [dripping dripped]

drive [driving drove driven]

drizzle [drizzling drizzled]

drone [droning droned]

drool [drooling drooled]

droop *[down] · droopy
  [drooping drooped]

drop *[let fall]

drore · draw *[pull, art]
  · drawer *[box]

drought

drove

drown [drowning drowned]

drowsy · drowsier

drowt · drought

drudge · drudgery

drue · drew

drug [drugging drugged]

drule · drool

drum [drumming drummed]

drunk · drunkenly

dry [dries drying dried]

dryer *[machine] · drier *[less wet]

dryve · drive

du · dew *[drops]
  · do *[get done]
  · due *[owing]

dual *[two] · duel *[fight]
  · jewel *[gem]

dub [dubbing dubbed]

dubbul · double

duchess · duchesses

duck [ducking ducked]

duckling

dud

due *[owed] · dew *[drops]
  · do *[get done]
  · Jew *[religion]

duel *[fight] · dual *[two]

duet

duffel coat

duke

dull · duller · dullness

dum · dumb

dumb · dumber · dumbest

dummy · dummies

dump [dumping dumped]

dumpling

dumpy   dumpier

dune

dung

dungarees

dungeon

dunjon   dungeon

duo

Dupiter   Jupiter

duplicate   duplication

  [duplicating duplicated]

during

durt   dirt

dury   jury

dusk   dusky   duskier

dust [dusting dusted]

dusty   dustier

dutiful   dutifully

duty   duties

duv   dove

duvay   duvet

duvet

duwel   dual *[two]

                 duel *[fight]

duz   does

duzn't   doesn't

duzzen   dozen

dwarf   dwarves

dwell [dwelling dwelled dwelt]

dworf   dwarf

Check out
di as well

dye *[colour]   die *[death]

dyeing *[colour]

dying *[death]

dylute   dilute

dynamic

dynamite

dynamo

dynasty

dynosaur   dinosaur

Dyoon   June

dysabul   disable

dysentery

dyslexia   dyslexic

dyspraxia   dyspraxic

Check out
dis as well

each

eager   eagerly   eagerness

eagle   eaglet

ear   ~ache ~phones ~plugs

ear   ~ring ~shot ~wig

eares   ears

early   earlier   earliest

earn *[money]   urn *[vase]
  [earning earned]

earnings

earth   earthly

earthquake

earthworm

eary   eerie *[scary]
               eyrie *[nest]

east   ~erly ~ern ~wards

Easter

easy   easier   easiest   easily

eat [eating ate eaten]

ebb [ebbing ebbed]

eccentric

ech   each

echo [echoes echoing echoed]

ecksact   exact

Check out
ex as well

ecksamin   examine

ecksaminashun examination

ecksampul   example

ecksceed   exceed

eckscite   excite

eclipse

ecology   ecologist

ecsentric   eccentric

eczema

edebul   edible

edge [edging edged]

edgy   edgier   edgiest

edible

edition *[copy]   addition *[sum]

edj   edge

educashun   education

education

eel

eer   ear

eerie *[scary]   eyrie *[nest]

eerily   eeriness

eese   ease

eest   east

Eester   Easter

eestern   eastern

eesy   easy

eet   eat

eeves   eaves

eezee   easy

efect	effect *[result]
	affect *[alter]
effect *[result]	affect *[alter]
effective	effectively
effectiveness	
efficiency	
efficient	efficiently
effort	
effortless	effortlessly
efishent	efficient
efishuncy	efficiency
efort	effort
eg	egg
ege	edge
egect	eject
eger	eager
egg [egging egged]	
egg	~cup ~shell
Egipshuns	Egyptians
egsact	exact

Check out
ex as well

egsaggerate	exaggerate
egsample	example
egul	eagle
Egyptians	
egzotic	exotic

Eiffel Tower	
eight *[number]	ate *[food]
eighteen	eighteenth
eighth	
eighty	eighties eightieth
eigt	eight
eigth	eighth
either	
eject [ejecting ejected]	
eji	edgy
ekcentrik	eccentric

Check out
ec as well

eko	echo
eksampul	example
eksentric	eccentric
eksma	eczema
ekwivalent	equivalent
elament	element
elastic	elasticity
Elastoplast™	
elavatid	elevated
elbow [elbowing elbowed]	
elder	elderly eldest
elderberry	elderberries
eldur	elder
election	

68

electric   electrical

electrically

electricity   electrician

electricle   electrical

electrify [electrifies]

  [electrifying electrified]

electrocute [electrocuted]

electrocution

electron

electronic   electronically

eleet   elite

elefant   elephant

elekshun   election

elektrik   electric

elektrisitee   electricity

element

elevate [elevated] elevator

eleven   eleventh

elf elves elfin elfish

eligible

eliminate [eliminating eliminated]

Elisabethun   Elizabethan

eliterashun   alliteration

Elizabethan

elk

elm

eloap   elope

elongated

elope [eloping eloped]

else ~where

elude [eluding eluded]

elushun   illusion

                   *[fantasy]

              allusion *[hint]

email

emarald   emerald

embalm [embalmed]

embankment

embarass   embarrass

embark [embarking embarked]

embarm   embalm

embarrass   embarrassment

  [embarrassing embarrassed]

embassy   embassies

embers

emblem

embrace [embracing embraced]

embrio   embryo

embroider [embroidered]

embroidery

embroyder   embroider

embryo

emerald

emerge [emerging emerged]

emergency   emergencies

emfasis   emphasis

emigrant *[exits] immigrant
*[arrives]

emigrate *[exit] immigrate
*[arrive]

[emigrating emigrated]

emigration   immigration
*[exit]   *[arrival]

emoshun   emotion

emotion

emotional   emotionally

emperor   empress

empire *[lands]   umpire *[game]

employ [employing employed]

employee   employer

employment

emprer   emperor

empty   emptier   emptiest

emrald   emerald

emtee   empty

emu

emurge   emerge

enabel   enable

enable [enabling enabled]

enamel

encampment

enchant enchantment
[enchanting enchanted]

enchantress

enciclopeedia   encyclopaedia

enclose [enclosing enclosed]

enclosure

encoar   encore

encore

encounter

[encountering encountered]

encourage   encouragement
[encouraging encouraged]

encownter   encounter

encyclopaedia   encyclopaedic

end [ending ended]

endanger
[endangering endangered]

endeavour
[endeavouring endeavoured]

endever   endeavour

endid   ended

endless   endlessly

endurance

endure [enduring endured]

enemy   enemies

energetic   energetically

energy   energies

enerjy   energy

enething   anything

enforce [enforcing enforced]

enforse   enforce

engage [engaging engaged]

engagement

Engerlish   English

engine

engineer   engineering

English

engrave [engraving engraved]

engraver

engrossed

engulf [engulfing engulfed]

enjine   engine

enjineer   engineer

enjoy [enjoying enjoyed]

enjoyable   enjoyably

enjoyment

enjure   endure

enkurage   encourage

enlarge [enlarging enlarged]

enlargement

enlist [enlisting enlisted]

enmie   enemy

enormous   enormously

enough

enquire   enquiry

enrage [enraged]

enrol [enrolling enrolled]

ensime   enzyme

ensure [ensuring ensured]

ensyclopeedia   encyclopaedia

entangle [entangled]

enter [entering entered]

enterprise   enterprising

entertain   entertainment
  [entertaining entertained]

enthoosiasum   enthusiasm

enthusiasm   enthusiast

enthusiastic enthusiastically

entire   entirely

entrance   entrant

entrust [entrusting entrusted]

entry   entries

entur   enter

enturtain   entertain

entyre   entire

enuff   enough

enurjetic   energetic

envee   envy

envelop *[surround]
  [enveloping enveloped]

envelope *[paper]

envie   envy

envious   enviously

enviroment   environment

environment

environmental

environmentally

envlope   envelope

envy [envies envying envied]

envyronment   environment

eny   any

enzyme

epic

epidemic

epilepsy   epileptic

episewd   episode

episode

epitaph

epitarf   epitaph

eqewstrian   equestrian

equal   equally
   [equalling equalled]

equalise   equaliser
   [equalising equalised]

equality   equalities

equation

equator   equatorial

equestrian

equilateral

equilibrium

equinox

equip   equipment
   [equipping equipped]

equivalent   equivalence

eqwpment   equipment

erase [erasing erased]

eratic   erratic

erer   error

erly   early

ernest   earnest

erode [eroding eroded]

erosion

errand

erratic   erratically

error

erth   earth

erupt [erupting erupted]

eruption

esay   essay

escalator

escape [escaping escaped]

eschuary   estuary

escort [escorting escorted]

esculator   escalator

esenshul   essential

eskape   escape

Eskimo

eskort   escort

especially

espinarj   espionage

espionage

essay

essential   essentially

establish   establishment
[establishing established]
estate
estchury   estuary
esteem [esteemed]
estern   eastern
estimate   estimation
[estimating estimated]
estuary   estuaries
esy   easy
eternal   eternally
eternity
ethnic
ethur   either
eturnity   eternity
euphemism
euro
European
Eurostar™
euthanasia
evacuate evacuation evacuee
[evacuating evacuated]
evade [evading evaded]
evaluate   evaluation
[evaluating evaluated]
evaporate   evaporation
[evaporating evaporated]
evasive

even   evenly   evenness
evenchualy   eventually
evening
event   eventful
eventual   eventually
ever   ~green ~lasting ~more
every   ~body ~day ~one
every   ~thing ~where
evict [evicting evicted]
eviction
evidence
evident   evidently
evikt   evict
evil   evilly
evning   evening
evolution
evolve [evolving evolved]
evon   even
evrewere   everywhere
evry   every
evur   ever
ewe *[sheep]   you *[person]
                      yew *[tree]
exact   exactly   exactness
exaggerate   exaggeration
[exaggerating exaggerated]
exale   exhale
exam   examination

examine [examining examined]

example

exasperate   exasperation
  [exasperating exasperated]

excavate   excavator
  [excavating excavated]

excavation

exceed [exceeding exceeded]

exceedingly

excel [excelling excelled]

excellence   excellent

excepshun   exception

except [but]   accept [take]

exception

exceptional   exceptionally

excercise   exercise

excershun   excursion

excess   excessively

exchange [exchanging exchanged]

excitable   excitability

excite *[thrill]   exit *[out]

excite   excitement

excited *[thrilled] exited *[left]

excitedly

exclaim [exclaiming exclaimed]

exclamation

exclude   exclusion
  [excluding excluded]

exclusive   exclusively

excrement

excrete   excretion
  [excreting excreted]

excursion

excuse [excusing excused]

excusable

excwiset   exquisite

execute [executing executed]

execution   executioner

executive

exekushun   execution

exekute   execute

exellent   excellent

exempt   exemption

exercise [exercising exercised]

exert [exerting exerted]

exertion

exhale [exhaling exhaled]

exhaust   exhaustion
  [exhausting exhausted]

exhibit   exhibitor
  [exhibiting exhibited]

exhibition

exhorst   exhaust

exibishun   exhibition

exibit   exhibit

exile [exiling exiled]

exist [existing existed]

existence   existent

exit *[out]   excite *[thrill]

exitement   excitement

exklude   exclude

exklusiv   exclusive

exkrement   excrement

exkurshun   excursion

exkuse   excuse

exkwisit   exquisite

exorcise [exorcising exorcised]

exorcist   exorcism

exotic

expand   expansion

  [expanding expanded]

expanse

expect   expectation

  [expecting expected]

expectant   expectantly

expectayshun   expectation

expedishun   expedition

expedition

expel [expelling expelled]

expence   expense

expense   expensive

experense   experience

experience

  [experiencing experienced]

experiment   experimentation

  [experimenting experimented]

experimental experimentally

expert   expertly

expertees   expertise

expertise

expire [expiring expired]

expiry

explain [explaining explained]

explanation   explanatory

exploar   explore

explode [exploding exploded]

exploit   exploitation

  [exploiting exploited]

exploration   exploratory

explore [exploring explored]

exploshun   explosion

explosion   explosive

exployt   exploit

export [exporting exported]

express [expressing expressed]

expression   expressionless

expressive   expressively

expulsion

expurt   expert

exquisite   exquisitely

exseed   exceed

exsel   excel

exsellense	excellence
exsept	except
exsert	exert
exsite	excite

extend [extending extended]

extension

extensive extensively

extent

extention	extension

exterior

exterminate exterminator
  [exterminating exterminated]

extermination

external externally

extinct extinction

extinguish [extinguishes]
  [extinguishing extinguished]

extra ~terrestrial

extract [extracting extracted]

extraordinarily

extraordinary

extravagance extravagant

extravagantly

extream	extreme

extreme extremely

extrordinary	extraordinary

extrovert

exturminate	exterminate
exturnal	external
exurcise	exercise
exurt	exert

eye ~brow ~lash

eye ~lid ~liner

eye ~sight ~witness

Eyemax	Imax™
eyether	either
eyrie *[nest]	eerie *[scary]

fable

fabric

fabulous

face *[head]

face *[look] [facing faced]

fachen   fashion

fact   factual

facter   factor

factor

factory   factories

facts *[true]   fax *[paper]

fad

fade [fading faded]

Fahrenheit

faik   fake

fail [failing failed]

failure

faint [fainting fainted]

faintly

fair *[event]   fare *[bus]

fair *[just]

fair   fairly   fairness

fair-haired

fairground

fairo   Pharoah

fairy *[sprite]   fairies

  ferry *[boat]

fairy-godmother

fairytale

faite   fate

faith   faithful   faithfully

fake [faking faked]

fakt   fact

faktoree   factory

falcon   falconry

fale   fail

fall [falling fell fallen]

false   falsely   falseness

famas   famous

fame   famed

familiar   familiarity

family   families

famine

famished

famous   famously

fan [fanning fanned]

fanatic

fancy [fancies]

fancy   fancier   fanciest

fanfare

fang

fansy   fancy

fantasise [fantasising fantasised]

fantastic   fantastically

fantasy   fantasies

fantisize   fantasise

fantisy   fantasy

fantom   phantom

far *[distant]   fare *[bus]

faraoh   Pharaoh

faraway

farce

fare *[bus]   fair *[event]

farewell

Far East [the]

Farenheight   Fahrenheit

far-fetched

Farisee   Pharisee

farm   ~land ~yard

farsen   fasten

farst   fast

fart [farting farted]

farther *[distant] father *[dad]

farthest

fary   fairy

fascinate   fascination
  [fascinating fascinated]

fase   face

fashion   fashionable

fashionably

fassinate   fascinate

fast [fasting fasted]

fasten [fastening fastened]

fast-forward

fat   fatter   fattest

fatal   fatally

fatality   fatalities

fate *[destiny]   fête *[festival]

fateful   fatefully

faten   fatten

father *[dad]   farther *[distant]

Father Christmas

fatherhood

father-in-law

fatherly

fatten [fattening fattened]

fatty   fattier   fattiest

fault   faulty   faultless

faun *[myths]   fawn *[deer]

fauna

favirite   favourite

favour   favourable

favourably

favourite   favouritism

favret   favourite

fawlt   fault

fawn *[colour, deer]

fax *[paper]   facts *[true]
  [faxing faxed]

fayr   fair *[just, event]

                   fare *[bus]

fayth   faith

faze *[bother]   phase *[stage]
  [fazed]

fead	feed
feal	feel
feald	field

fear [fearing feared]

fearful   fearfully

fearless   fearlessly

feasant	pheasant

feast [feasting feasted]

feat *[action]   feet *[toes]

feather feathered feathery

featherweight

feature [featuring featured]

Febrary	February
February	
Febuery	February
fech	fetch
fed	
feeblely	feebly
feechure	featur

feed [feeding fed]

feel [feeling felt]

feeld	field
feeler	
feend	fiend
feer	fear
feerse	fierce

feest	feast

feet *[toes]   feat *[action]

feetus	foetus
feild	field
feind	fiend
feirce	fierce
fell	
fellow	

felt   felt-tip

female

femenin	feminine

feminine

feminist   feminism

fence [fencing fenced]

fend [fending fended]

ferm	firm

ferment [fermenting fermented]

fern

fernish	furnish
ferniture	furniture

ferocious   ferociously

feroshus	ferocious

ferret [ferreting ferreted]

Ferris wheel

ferry   ferries

ferst	first
ferther	further
ferthest	furthest

fertile

fertilise   fertilisation
 [fertilising fertilised]

fertility

festival

festive   festivities

fetch [fetching fetched]

fête *[festival]   fate *[destiny]

fether   feather

feud [feuding feuded]

feudal   feudalism

fever

feverish   feverishly

few *[not many]   phew
                   *[exclamation]

fewgitiv   fugitive

fewl   fuel

fewneral   funeral

fewse   fuse

fezant   pheasant

fial   file

fiancé *[man]

fiancée *[lady]

fianl   final

fiansay   fiancé *[man]
                   fiancée *[lady]

fiar   fire

fib [fibbing fibbed]

fibre   fibreglass

fibur   fibre

ficks   fix

fickst   fixed

ficshun   fiction

fiction   fictional

fiddle [fiddling fiddled]

fiddly   fiddliest

fidget   fidgety [fidgeting fidgeted]

field [fielding fielded]

field   ~mouse ~work

fiend   fiendish   fiendishly

fier   fear *[afraid]
                   fire *[flame]

fierce   fiercer   fiercest

fiercely   fierceness

fierse   fierce

fiery   fierier   fieriest

fif   five

fiftee   fifty

fifteen   fifteenth

fifth

fifty   fifties   fiftieth

fig

figer   figure

figerativ   figurative

figet   fidget

fight [fighting fought]

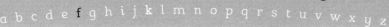

figurative

figure [figuring figured]

fiksed   fixed

fikshun   fiction

file [filing filed]

fill [filling filled]

fillet

filly   fillies

film [filming filmed]

filosofer   philosopher

filth   filthier   filthiest

filthy

fimail   female

fin *[fish]   Finn *[person]

final *[last]   finally

finale *[last event]

finalist

finarlay   finale

finck   think

find [finding found]

finder

fine [fining fined]

finely

finerly   finally

finger [fingering fingered]

finger   ~nail ~print

finish [finishing finished]

finly   finally

Finn *[person]   fin *[fish]

finsh   finish *[end]

fiord

fir *[tree]   fur *[coat]

fire [firing fired]

fire   ~arm ~brigade

fire extinguisher

fire   ~place ~work

firm firmer firmest

firmly

firn   fern

firry   furry

first   firstly

firsty   thirsty

firther   further

firtile   fertile

firy   fiery

fish [fishing fished]

fisher   fisherman

fishy

fisical   physical

fisics   physics

fist

fit *[clothes]   fight *[hit]
   [fitting fitted]

fit *[strong]   fitness

fite   fight

fiv   five

five

fix [fixes fixing fixed]

fixture

fizz [fizzes fizzing fizzed]

fizzle [fizzling fizzled]

fizzy   fizzier   fizziest

fjord

flabby   flabbier   flabbiest

flag [flagging flagged]

flake [flaking flaked]

flame [flaming flamed]

flamingo

flan

flannel

flap [flapping flapped]

flare [flaring flared]

flash [flashes flashing flashed]

flash   ~back   ~light

flashy   flashier   flashiest

flask

flat flatter flattest flatly

flatten [flattening flattened]

flatter   flattery
   [flattering flattered]

flaunt [flaunting flaunted]

flaver   flavour

flavour [flavouring flavoured]

flaw *[fault]   floor *[base]

flawed   flawless

flea *[insect]   flee *[run]

flecks *[dots]   flex *[bend]

flecksibul   flexible

fledgling

flee *[run]   flea *[insect]
   [fleeing fled]

fleece [fleecing fleeced]

fleet

flert   flirt

flesh   fleshy

flew *[flight]   flu *[ill]

flewid   fluid

flex *[bend]   flecks *[dots]
   [flexes flexing flexed]

flexible   flexibility

flick [flicking flicked]

flicker [flickering flickered]

flick-knife   flick-knives

flies

flight *[trip]   flit *[dash]

fliing   flying

flimsy   flimsier   flimsiest

flinch [flinches flinching flinched]

fling [flinging flung]

flint   flinty

flip [flipping flipped]

flippant   flippantly

flipper

flirt [flirting flirted]

flisse   fleece

flit *[dash]   flight *[trip]

float [floating floated]

flock [flocking flocked]

floe *[ice]   flow *[river]

flog [flogging flogged]

flood [flooding flooded]

floor *[base]   flaw *[fault]

floot   flute

flop [flopping flopped]

floppy   floppier   floppiest

floral   florist

flornt   flaunt

floss

flote   float

flour *[food]   flower *[bud]

flourish [flourishes]
  [flourishing flourished]

flow *[river]   floe *[ice]
  [flowing flowed]

flower *[plant]   flour *[food]
  [flowering flowered]

flown

flox   flocks

flu *[ill]   flew *[fly]

flud   flood

fluent   fluently

fluff

fluffy   fluffier   fluffiest

fluid

fluke

flume

flung

fluorescent light

flurish   flourish

flush [flushing flushed]

flustered

flute

flutter [fluttering fluttered]

fly *[insect, travel]   flies

fly [flies flying flew flown]

foal

foam [foaming foamed]

fobia   phobia

focus [focuses focusing focused]

fodder

foe

foetus   foetal

fog   foggy

foil [foiling foiled]

foke   folk

foks   fox

fokus   focus

fold [folding folded]

fole	foal	fore	~arm ~cast ~ground	
folk	~lore	fore	~hand ~head ~most	
foll	fall	foreboding		
follow	follower	foreign	foreigner	
[following followed]		foren	foreign	
fome	foam	foresee [foresaw foreseen]		
fon	phone	forest	forestation	
fond fonder fondest fondly		forester	forestry	
fone	phone	foretell	foretold	
fonic	phonic	forever		
font		forfeit		
food *[eat]	feud *[fight]	forfit	forfeit	
fool [fooling fooled]		forgave		
foolish	foolishly	forge [forging forged]		
foot	~note ~path ~print	forgery	forgeries	
foot	~step ~wear ~work	forget [forgetting forgot]		
football	footballer	forgetful	forgetfulness	
for *[use]	fore *[front]	forgive [forgiving forgave forgiven]		
	four *[number]	forgiveness		
forbid		forgot	forgotten	
[forbidding forbade forbidden]		forj	forge	
forcast	forecast	fork [forking forked]		
force [forcing forced]		forlt	fault	
forceful	forcefully	form [forming formed]		
forchoon	fortune	formal		
ford		formashun	formation	
fore *[front]	for *[use]	format [formatting formatted]		
	four *[number]	formation		

former   formerly

formula   formulas   formulae

forn   faun *[myths]
                  fawn *[deer]

forna   fauna

forrest   forest

forse   force

fort *[castle]   fought *[hit]
                  thought *[think]

forteen   fourteen

forthcoming

fortnight   fortnightly

fortunate   fortunately

fortune

forty   fortieth

forward   forwards

fossil fossilise [fossilised]

foster [fostering fostered]

foto   photo

Check out
ph as well

fotograf   photograph

fotosynthesis   photosynthesis

fought *[hit]   fort *[castle]
                  thought *[think]

foul *[dirty]   fowl *[bird]

fouler   foulest

found [founding founded]

foundation

fountain

four *[number]   for *[use]
                  fore *[front]

Check out
for as well

fourbid   forbid

fource   force

fourhand   forehand

fourmula   formula

fourt   fought *[hit]
                  fort *[castle]
                  thought *[think]

fourteen   fourteenth

fourth *[4th]   forth *[on]

fourtnight   fortnight

fowl *[bird]   foul *[dirty]

fownd   found

fowntain   fountain

fox   foxes

foyl   foil

fraction

fracture [fracturing fractured]

frael   frail

fragile

fragment

fragrance   fragrant

fragrense   fragrance

frail   frailer   frailest

frajile   fragile

fraksher   fracture

frakshun   fraction

frale   frail

frame [framing framed]

frank frankly frankness

frankfurter

frankincense

frantic   frantically

frase   phrase

fraud   fraudster

fraught

freak   freakish

freckle   freckled

free [freeing freed]

freedom

freer   freest   freely

freestyle

freeze *[ice]   frieze *[strip]
   [freezing froze frozen]

freezer

freind   friend

frekwency   frequency

frekwent   frequent

french

french fries

frend   friend

frens   friends

frenzy   frenzied

frequency   frequencies

frequent   frequently

fresh   fresher   freshest

freshen [freshening freshened]

freshly   freshness

fret *[mope]   threat *[warn]
   [fretting fretted]

frew   threw *[ball]
          through *[go
                through]

friar   friary

frickshun   friction

friction

Friday

fridge

fried

friend   ~less ~ship

friendly friendlier friendliest

frieze *[strip]   freeze *[ice]

frigate

frige   fridge

fright *[fear]

frighten [frightening frightened]

frightful   frightfully

frill   frilly   frilliest

fringe   fringed

Frisbee™

frisk [frisking frisked]

frisky   friskier   friskiest

fritter [frittering frittered]

frivolous

frizzy   frizzier   frizziest

frog   ~man ~spawn

frogmarch [frogmarched]

frolic [frolicked frolicking]

from

frong   throng

front

frontier

froot   fruit

frord   fraud

frorght   fraught

frost [frosting frosted]

frostbite   frostbitten

frosty   frostier   frostiest

froth [frothing frothed]

frothy

frown [frowning frowned]

froze   frozen

fruit

fruitful   fruitfulness

fruitless   fruitlessly

fruity   fruitier   fruitiest

frunt   front

fruntier   frontier

frustrate   frustration
  [frustrating frustrated]

frut   fruit

fry   [frying fried]

fryer   frying pan

fryt   fright

fucher   future

fud   food

fude   feud

fudge

fue   few

fuel [fuelling fuelled]

fugitive

ful   fool *[idiot]

               full *[complete]

fule   fuel

fulfil [fulfilling fulfilled]

full *[up]   fool *[idiot]

fullness   fully

fumble [fumbling fumbled]

fume [fuming fumed]

fun

function [functioning functioned]

fund [funding funded]

funeral

fungus   fungi

funkshun   **function**

funnel

funny   funnier   funniest

fur *[coat]   fir *[tree]

furious   furiously

furn   **fern**

furnace

furnish [furnishes]
   [furnishing furnished]

furniture

furoshus   **ferocious**

furry *[hairy]   **fury** *[anger]*

furrier   furriest

furst   **first**

further   furthest

furthering

furthermore

furtile   **fertile**

furtilise   **fertilise**

fury *[anger]   **furry** *[hairy]*

fuse [fusing fused]

fuss *[worry]   fuzz *[fluff]*
   [fusses fussing fussed]

fussy   fussier   fussiest

fut   **foot**

future

fuzz

fuzzy   fuzzier   fuzziest

fyfty   **fifty**

fynd   **find**

fysical   **physical**

fysics   **physics**

fyve   **five**

Check out
fi as well

gabble [gabbling gabbled]

gadget

gael   gale

gag [gagging gagged]

gage   gauge

gaggle

gaily

gain [gaining gained]

gaip   gape

gajet   gadget

gala

galaxy   galactic

gale   gale-force

galery   gallery

galleon

gallery   galleries

galley

gallon

gallop [galloping galloped]

gallows

galy   gaily *[merrily]

         galley *[ship]

gamble *[games]

   [gambling gambled]

gambol *[frolic]

   [gambolling gambolled]

game

gammon

gander

gang   ~plank ~way

gangly

gangster

gap *[space]   gap-toothed

gape *[look, open] [gaping gaped]

garage

garantey   guarantee

garbage

gard   guard

garden   gardening

gardian   guardian

gargle *[throat] [gargling gargled]

gargoyle *[carving]

garige   garage

garland

garlic   garlicky

garment

garrison

gas

gase   gaze

gash   gashes

gasp [gasping gasped]

gastly   ghastly

gate

gateau   gateaux

gatecrash   gatecrasher

gather [gathering gathered]

gattoe	gateau	gentle	gentleness
gaugius	gorgeous	gentleman	
gave		genuine	genuinely
gawky		geography	
gayn	gain	geology	geologist
gayt	gate	geometry	
gaze [gazing gazed]		geranium	
gear ~box ~stick		gerbil	
geek geeky		gergle	gurgle
geese		geriatric	
gel		gerila	gorilla
gelignite		gerl	girl
gelly	jelly	germ	
gem		German	
Gemini		germinate germination	
gender		[germinating germinated]	
general		gess	guess
generation		gest	guessed
generosity			*[estimated]
generous generously			guest *[visitor]
genes *[DNA] jeans *[denim]		gesture	
genetic		get [getting got]	
genetic engineering		getto	ghetto
genetically modified		gewel	jewel
genie			
genius			
genral	general		
gent		gewelry	jewellery

Check out
je as well

gewish	Jewish	
geyser		
ghastly	ghastliest	
ghetto	ghetto blaster	
ghost	ghostly	
ghoul	ghoulish	
giant		
gibbering	gibberish	
gidanse	guidance	
giddy	giddiness	
gide	guide	
gier	gear	
gift		
gig *[show]	jig *[dance]	
gigabyte		
gigantic		
giggle *[ha ha]	jiggle *[jog]	
gilotine	guillotine	
gilt *[gold]	guilt *[shame]	
giltey	guilty	
gin		
ginee pig	guinea pig	
ginger	gingerly	gingery
gingham		
giraffe		
girgul	gurgle	
girl	girlfriend	girlie
giro *[bank]	gyro *[spins]	

gise	guise	
gist *[idea]	jest *[joke]	
gitar	guitar	
give [giving gave given]		
giy	guy	
Giy Forks	Guy Fawkes	
glacier	glacial	
glad	gladly	gladness
gladiator		
glaisha	glacier	
glamour	glamorous	
glance [glancing glanced]		
gland	glandular fever	
glare [glaring glared]		
glarnse	glance	
glars	glass	
glass	glasses	glassful
glazier		
gleam [gleaming gleamed]		
glide [gliding glided]		
glimmer [glimmering]		
glimpse [glimpsed]		
glimsped	glimpsed	
glint		
glisten [glistening glistened]		
glitter [glittering glittered]		
gloat [gloating gloated]		
global	globally	

globe

gloom   gloomy

gloomier   gloomiest

glossy   glossier   glossiest

glove

glow   glow-worm

glucose

glue [gluing glued]

glutton

gnarled

gnat

gnaw *[bite]   nor *[neither]
  [gnawing gnawed]

gnome   gnomish

go [goes going went]

go   go-kart

goal   goalie   goalkeeper

goat

gob   ~smacked ~stopper

gobble [gobbling gobbled]

gobbledegook

goblin

God

god   ~dess ~child ~daughter

god   ~father ~mother ~parent

god   ~send ~son

goggle [goggling goggled]

goggle-eyed

gold   ~fish ~mine

golden

golf   golf course

gon   gone

gone   goner

good goodness

goodbye

Good Friday

gooey

gool   ghoul

goose   goose pimples

gooseberry   gooseberries

gorge [gorging gorged]

gorgeous

gorilla

gory   goriest

gosling

gospel

gossip

gost   ghost

got

goul   ghoul

government

gowing   going

grab [grabbing grabbed]

grace   graceful   gracefully

grade

gradual   gradually

92

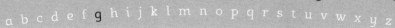

graf	graph
graffiti	
graid	grade
grail	
grain	grainy
gram	
grammar	
grammatically	
granade	grenade
granchild	grandchild
grand	~child ~children
grand	~daughter ~father
grand	~ma ~mother ~pa
grand	~parent ~son ~stand
grandad	
granny	grannies
graph	
grapple [grappling grappled]	
gras	grass
grase	grace *[goodness]
	graze *[feed, cut]
grasp [grasping grasped]	
grass	grassy grasshopper
grate *[fire]	great *[big]
grateful	gratefully
grater *[cheese]	greater *[bigger]
gratest	greatest
gratichewd	gratitude

gratitude

grave	gravely
grave	~digger ~stone ~yard
gravel	gravelly
gravity	
gravy	
gray	grey
grayn	grain
graze	
grdon	garden
grease	~paint ~proof
greasy	
great *[big]	grate *[fire]
greater	
greatly	greatness
greed	greedier greediest
greedy	greedily
green	greenery
green	~grocer ~house
greenhouse	
greese	grease
greet	greetings
greif	grief
greive	grieve
gremlin	
gren	green
grenade	
grew	

grewsome   gruesome

grey ~hound

grief grief-stricken

grieve [grieving grieved]

grill [grilling grilled]

grim *[bad]*

grime *[dirt]*

grimy grimiest

grin [grinning grinned]

grind [grinding ground]

grip [gripping gripped]

grit gritty

grizzly

groan *[moan]*   grown *[up]*
[groaning groaned]

grocer groceries grocery

groggy groggier

grone   groan *[moan]*
                  grown *[up]*

groom

groop   group

groosum   gruesome

groove *[slot]*   grove *[trees]*

grope [groping groped]

groser   grocer

gross grossly

grotto grottos

grotty grottier grottiest

ground ~less ~sheet ~sman

group

grouse

grove *[wood]*   groove *[slot]*

grovel [grovelling grovelled]

grow growing

growl [growling growled]

grown *[up]*   groan *[moan]*

grownd   ground

growth

grub

grubby grubbier grubbiest

grudge grudgingly

grue   grew

gruesome

gruff gruffly

gruge   grudge

grumble [grumbling grumbled]

grumpy grumpier
  grumpiest

grunt [grunting grunted]

grupe   group

guarantee guarantees
  [guaranteeing guaranteed]

guard guardsman

guardian

gud   good

guess [guessing guessed]

guessed *[estimated]

guest *[visitor]

guidance

guide   ~book ~lines

  [guiding guided]

guillotine

guilt *[shame]   gilt *[gold]

guilty guiltier guiltiest

guinea pig

guitar guitarist

gulf   Gulf stream

gull

gully gullies

gulp [gulping gulped]

gum   ~shield

gun   ~boat ~dog ~fight ~fire

gun   ~man ~point ~powder

gun   ~ship ~shot

gurbil   gerbil

gurgle [gurgling gurgled]

gurl   girl

guseberry   gooseberry

gush   [gushes gushing gushed]

gust   gusty

gutter   guttering

guvern   govern

guverment   government

guy   Guy Fawkes

guzzle [guzzling guzzled]

gym   gymnasium

gymkhana

gymnast   gymnastics

gypsy   gypsies

H-bomb

habit

habitat   habitation

hack [hacking hacked]

hackles

hacksaw

had   hadn't [had not]

haev   have

haf   have

hag   haggard

haggis

haggle [haggling haggled]

hail [hailing hailed]

hailstone

hair *[head]   hare *[animal]

hair   ~brush ~cut ~dresser

hairy   hairier   hairiest

half   halves

half   ~hour ~way

hall *[room]   haul *[pull]

hall   ~mark ~way

Halloween

hallucinate   hallucination
   [hallucinating hallucinated]

halo   haloes

halt [halting halted]

halve [halving halved]

ham   ~burger

hammer [hammering hammered]

hammock

hamster

hand [handing handed]

hand   ~bag ~book ~ful

hand   ~made ~shake ~stand

handcuff [handcuffed]

handicap [handicapped]

handkerchief   hanky

handle [handling handled]

handsome   handsomest

handwriting   handwritten

handy   handier   handiest

handyman

hang [hanging hung]

hangar *[plane]

hanger *[clothes]

hankercheif   handkerchief

hankuff   handcuff

hanriting   handwriting

hanshake   handshake

hansome   handsome

hapand   happened

haphazard   haphazardly

hapon   happen

hapond   happened

happen [happening happened]

happy   happier   happiest

harbour

hard   harder   hardest

hard   ~board ~ship

harden [hardening hardened]

hardly   hardness

hardy   hardier   hardiest

hare *[animal]   hair *[head]

harf   half

harm [harming harmed]

harmful   harmfully

harmless   harmlessly

harmony   harmonies

harness   harnesses

[harnessing harnessed]

harp   harpist

harpoon [harpooned]

harrier jet

harsh   harsher   harshest

harshly   harshness

hartless   heartless

harvest [harvesting harvested]

has   hasn't [has not]

hassle [hassling hassled]

haste

hasty   hastier   hastiest

hat *[head]   hate *[dislike]

hatch [hatches hatching hatched]

hatchet

hate *[dislike]   hat *[head]

[hating hated]

hateful

hath   have

hatred

haul *[pull]   hall *[room]

[hauling hauled]

haunches

haunt [haunting haunted]

have [has having had]

haven

haven't [have not]

havoc

hawk

hawse   hoarse *[voice]

horse *[animal]

hay *[grass]   hey *[greet]

hay   ~stack ~wire

hayl   hail *[ice]

hazard

haze hazy hazier hazily

hazel

he   he's [he is, has]

head [heading headed]

headache

head   ~dress ~light ~line

head   ~master ~mistress

head   ~phones ~quarters

heal *[cure]   heel *[foot]
[healing healed]
healer
health   healthy   healthily
healthier   healthiest
heap [heaping heaped]
hear *[sound]   here *[place]
[hearing heard]
heard *[ear]   herd *[animals]
hearse
heart   ~beat ~breaking
heart   ~broken
heartily
heartless   heartlessly
hearty   heartier   heartiest
heat [heating heated] heater
heather
heave [heaving heaved]
heaven   heavenly
heavily   heaviness
heavy   heavier   heaviest
Hebrew
hectare
hectic
he'd [he had, would]
hed   head
hedge [hedging hedged]
hedge   ~hog ~row

heds   heads
heel *[foot]   he'll *[he will]
heer   hear
heffer   heifer
hefty   heftier   heftiest
heifer
height
heighten [heightened]
heir *[inherits]   hair *[head]
heiress   heirloom
heksagon   hexagon
held
helicopter   helipad   heliport
helium
he'll [he will, shall]
hell *[devil]   heel *[foot]
hello *[greet]   halo *[light]
helm   helmsman
helmet
help [helping helped]
helper   helpful   helpfully
helpfulness
helpless   helplessly
helplessness
helter-skelter
helth   health
hemisphere
hen   ~pecked

her *[female]   here *[place]

herald [heralding heralded]

herb   herbal

herbivore   herbivorous

herd *[animals]   heard *[ear]
  [herding herded]

herdul   hurdle

here *[place]   hear *[sound]

herl   hurl

hermit   hermitage

hero   heroes

heroic   heroically

heroine

heroism

heron

herry   hairy

hers *[she owns]

herself

hert   hurt

hertul   hurtle

hesitant   hesitantly

hesitate   hesitation
  [hesitating hesitated]

heven   heaven

hevy   heavy

hexagon   hexagonal

hey *[greet]   hay *[grass]

hi *[greet]   high *[tall]

hibernate   hibernation
  [hibernating hibernated]

hiccup [hiccupping hicupped]

hid *[past of hide]

hide *[not seen]   [hiding]
  [hid, hidden]

hideous   hideously

hidrolik   hydraulic

hieght   height

hiena   hyena

hier   hear *[sound]

               here *[place]

               higher *[taller]

               hire *[employ]

hieroglyphics

hiest   highest

higeen   hygiene

higgledy-piggledy

high *[tall]   hi *[greet]

high   ~chair ~lands ~lighter

higher *[taller]   hire *[employ]

highest   highly

highlight [highlighting highlighted]

Highness

hights   heights

highway   ~man ~men

hijack   hijacker
  [highjacking highjacked]

99

hike [hiking hiked]

hilarious

hill ~side

hilly hillier hilliest

hilt

him *[male]   hymn *[song]

himself

hind ~quarters ~sight

hinder [hindering hindered]

Hindu Hinduism

hinge [hinging hinged]

hint [hinting hinted]

hip

hiper   hyper

hippopotamus

hir   her *[female]

    hire *[employ]

hirdel   hurdle

hire *[employ]   higher *[taller]

    [hiring hired]

hirl   hurl

his *[he owns]

hiss *[sound]   hisses

    [hissing hissed]

histeria   hysteria

histerical   hysterical

historian

historic historical

history histories

hit [hitting hit]   hitter

hitch [hitches hitching hitched]

hitch-hike   hitch-hiker

    [hitch-hiking hitch-hiked]

hite   height

hiten   heighten

hive

hiway   highway

hiy   high

ho *[shout]   hoe *[dig]

hoaks   hoax

hoal   whole

hoard *[store]   horde *[mass]

    [hoarding hoarded]

hoarse *[voice]   horse *[ride]

hoarsely   hoarseness

hoax   hoaxes

    [hoaxing hoaxed]

hobble [hobbling hobbled]

hobby   hobbies

hockey

hoe *[dig]   ho *[shout]

    [hoeing hoed]

hog [hogging hogged]

Hogmanay

hoist [hoisting hoisted]

hokey   hockey

hold [holding held]   holder
hole *[gap]   whole *[full]
holey *[holes]   holy *[sacred]
                    wholly *[fully]
holiday
holier   holiest
hollow [hollowing hollowed]
holly *[tree]   holy *[sacred]
                    wholly *[fully]
Hollywood
holocaust
hologram
holster
holy *[sacred]   holly *[tree]
                    wholly *[fully]
homage
home   homely
homeless   homelessness
home-made
homesick   homesickness
homework
homige   homage
homonym
homophone
honer   honour
honest   honestly   honesty
honey   ~comb ~moon ~suckle
honk [honking honked]

honour [honouring honoured]
honourable   honourably
hood   hooded
hoof   hooves
hook [hooking hooked]
hooligan   hooliganism
hoop *[circle]   whoop *[shout]
hoot [hooting hooted]
hooter
hoover™ [hoovering hoovered]
hop *[jump]   hope *[wish]
  [hopping hopped]
hope [hoping hoped]
hopeful   hopefully
hopeless   hopelessly
hopital   hospital
hopskotch
horde *[mass]   hoard *[store]
horer   horror
horibul   horrible
horid   horrid
horific   horrific
horizon
horizontal   horizontally
hork   hawk
horl   hall *[room]
                  haul *[pull]
hormone

horn horned

hornches   haunches

hornet

hornt   haunt

horor   horror

horoscope

horrible horribly

horrid horridly

horrific horrifically

horrify [horrifies]

  [horrifying horrified]

horror

horse *[animal]   hoarse *[voice]

horse   ~fly ~hair ~power

horse   ~shoe ~whip

horthorn   hawthorn

hose *[water]   hoes *[digs]

hosed

hospital

host [hosting hosted]

hostage

hostel

hostess hostesses

hostile

hostility hostilities

hot hotter hottest hotly

hotel

hot-tempered

houes   house

hound [hounding hounded]

hour *[time]   our *[owns]

hourly

hours *[time]   ours *[owns]

hourse   hours

house [housing housed]

house   ~ful ~hold ~keeper

house   ~plant ~proud

house-trained

housewife housework

House of Commons

House of Lords

hovel

hover [hovering hovered]

how *[how much] who *[?]

however

howl [howling howled]

hownd   hound

howse   house

hoyst   hoist

hu   who *[?]

huch   hutch

hud   hood

huddle [huddling huddled]

huff

hug *[clasp]   huge *[large]

  [hugging hugged]

hugely hugeness

huj   huge

huligan   hooligan

hulk hulking

hull

hum [humming hummed]

human *[person]

humane *[caring] humanely

humble humbly

humbug

humer   humour

humid humidity

humiliate humiliation
  [humiliating humiliated]

humility

humorous

humour [humouring humoured]

hump ~back

hunch hunches
  [hunching hunched]

hundred hundredth

huney   honey

hung

hunger hungrier hungriest

hungry hungrily

hunk

hunny   honey

hunt [hunting hunted]

hunter

huntsman

hurbivor   herbivore

Check out **her** as well

hurd   heard *[sound]
                    herd *[animals]

hurdle [hurdling hurdled]

huriball   horrible

hurikane   hurricane

hurl [hurling hurled]

hurmit   hermit

hurray

hurricane

hurry hurriedly
  [hurries hurrying hurried]

hurse   hearse

hurt [hurting hurt]

hurtful

hurtle [hurtling hurtled]

husband

hush [hushed]

husk

husky huskier huskiest

hussel   hustle

hustle [hustling hustled]

hut

hutch	hutches
huver	hoover™
hy	hi
hybernate	hibernate

Check out
hi as well

hyde	hide
hydraulic	
hydrogen	
hyena	
hyer	higher *[taller]
	hire *[employ]
hyest	highest
hygiene	hygienist
hygienic	
hyjack	hijack
hyke	hike

hymn *[song]	him *[male]
hynd	hind
hyper	~active ~market
hyphen	
hypnosis	hypnotic
hypnotise [hypnotising hypnotised]	
hypnotist	hypnotism
hypochondria	hypochondriac
hypocrisy	hypocrite
hypotenuse	
hypothermia	
hyre	higher *[taller]
	hire *[employ]
hysteria	hysterics
hysterical	hysterically
hyt	height
hyway	highway

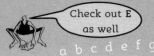
I *[me]   eye *[see]

ice *[cold]   eyes *[see]
  [icing iced]

iceberg

icee   icy

ich   itch

icicle

iclispe   eclipse

iconomy   economy

icy icier iciest

icycul   icicle

I'd [I had, would]

idea

ideal ideally

idear   idea

identical identically

identify [identified]

identity identities

idiot idiotic

idle *[lazy]   idol *[worship]

idly

idolise [idolising idolised]

idyllic

idyot   idiot

iether   either *[or]

if

igloo

ignerence   ignorance

ignition

ignor   ignore

ignorance ignorant

ignore [ignoring ignored]

ignorens   ignorance

ignorent   ignorant

iject   eject

iland   island

ilastic   elastic

ile   aisle *[passage]
                isle *[island]

I'le   I'll *[I will, shall]

ilegal   illegal

ilegibul   illegible

I'll *[I will, shall]   isle *[island]
                aisle *[walk]

ill iller illest

illegal illegally

illegible illegibly

illness

illuminations

illustrate illustrator
  [illustrating illustrated]

illustration

ilope   elope

ilustrashun   illustration

I'm [I am]

imaculate   immaculate

image   imagery

imaginary [imagining imagined]

imagination   imaginative

imagine   imaginable

imature   immature

imedeate   immediate

imens   immense

imerse   immerse

imige   image

imigrate   immigrate

imitate imitation imitator

  [imitating imitated]

immaculate   immaculately

immature   immaturity

immediate   immediately

immense   immensely

immigrant *[in] emigrant *[out]

immigrate *[in] emigrate *[out]

immigration   emigration

                *[in]   *[out]

immobile

immoral

immortal   immortality

immoshun   emotion

immune   immunity

immunise [immunised]

imorul   immoral

imp   impish

impact

impale [impaled]

impashens   impatience

impatience

impatient   impatiently

impechuous   impetuous

impede [impeding impeded]

imperfect   imperfectly

impersonate

  [impersonating impersonated]

impersonation   impersonator

impertinence   impertinent

impervious

impetuous   impetuously

implament   implement

implication

implore [imploring implored]

imply   implication

  [implying implied]

impolite   impoliteness

import [importing imported]

importance

important   importantly

impose [imposing imposed]

impossible   impossibly

impossibul   impossible

impostor

impourtant   important

impractical

impresiv   impressive

impress [impressing impressed]

impression   impressionable

impressionism   impressionist

impressive   impressively

imprison [imprisoned]

imprisonment

improbable

improper   improperly

impropur   improper

improve [improving improved]

improvement

improvise   improvisation

  [improvising improvised]

impruve   improve

impulse

impulsive   impulsively

impulsiveness

impure

impursonate   impersonate

impurtinents   impertinence

imunise   immunise

in *[go in]   inn *[pub]

inability

inaccessible

inaccurate   inaccurately

inacsessibul   inaccessible

inactive   inactivity

inacurate   inaccurate

inadequate   inadequately

inaksessible   inaccessible

inaktivity   inactivity

inappropriate   inappropriately

inattentive

inbarits   embarrassed

in-between

incapable

incense [incensed]

incensitiv   insensitive

incentive

incequre   insecure

incesant   incessant

incessant   incessantly

inch   inches

inchuitiv   intuitive

incident   incidentally

incignificant   insignificant

incincere   insincere

incision

incist   insist

incline   inclination

  [inclining inclined]

include   inclusion

  [including included]

incoherent

income   incoming

incompatible

incompetence

incompetent   incompetently

incomplete   incompletely

inconceivable   inconceivably

inconcistent   inconsistent

inconclusive

inconsiderate

inconsiderit   inconsiderate

inconsistency   inconsistencies

inconsistent   inconsistently

inconsolable

inconspicuous

inconspicuously

inconvenient

incorrect   incorrectly

increase   increasingly

  [increasing increased]

incredible   incredibly

incubate   incubator

  [incubating incubated]

incubation

incurable   incurably

indecent   indecently

indecisive

indeed

indefinite   indefinitely

indeks   index

independence

independent   independently

inderstre   industry

indescribable   indescribably

indesent   indecent

indesisiv   indecisive

indestructible

index   indices [indexing indexed]

Indian

indicate   indication

  [indicating indicated]

indicator

indicision   indecision

indigestion   indigestible

indignant

indigo

indijestion   indigestion

indikate   indicate

indikayshun   indication

indirect   indirectly

indiscreet   indiscretion

indiscribabul   indescribable

indisputable

indistinct   indistinctly

indistructabul   indestructible

individual   individually

individuality

indoor   indoors

indulge   indulgence

[indulging indulged]

indulgent

industree   industry

industrial

industrious   industriously

industry   industries

indyrect   indirect

ineckspensiv   inexpensive

inecksperiens   inexperience

inedible

inefectiv   ineffective

ineffective   ineffectively

inefficiency

inefficient   inefficiently

inekscusabul   inexcusable

inekspensiv   inexpensive

ineksperience   inexperience

inept   ineptly

inequality   inequalities

iner   inner

inescapable   inescapably

inevitability

inevitable   inevitably

inexcusable

inexpensive   inexpensively

inexperience   inexperienced

inexplicable   inexplicably

infachuated   infatuated

infamous   infamously

infancy

infant   infantile

infantry

infatuated   infatuation

infect [infecting infected]

infection

infectious   infectiously

infekshus   infectious

infekt   infect

infent   infant

infentry   infantry

infer [inferring inferred]

inference

inferior   inferiority

inferno

infertile   infertility

infest [infested]

infidel

infidelity   infidelities

infinite   infinitely

infinitee   infinity

infinitive

infinity

infirier   inferior

infirno   inferno

inflamabul   inflammable

inflame inflammable
  [inflaming inflamed]

inflammation

inflashun   inflation

inflate inflatable
  [inflating inflated]

inflation

inflaym   inflame

inflayt   inflate

inflewnce   influence

inflexible

inflict [inflicting inflicted]

influence [influencing influenced]

influenshall   influential

influential

inform informative
  [informing informed]

informal informality

informally

informant

informashun   information

information

infrared

infrequent infrequently

infuriate [infuriating infuriated]

ingenious ingeniously

ingenuity

ingrained

ingratitude

ingredient

ingreedyent   ingredient

ingury   injury

inhabit inhabitant
  [inhabiting inhabited]

inhail   inhale

inhalation

inhale [inhaling inhaled]

inherit [inherited]

inheritance

inhibit inhibition
  [inhibiting inhibited]

inhospitable

inings   innings

inishiate   initiate

inishul   initial

initial initially

initiate initiation
  [initiating initiated]

initiative

inject injection
  [injecting injected]

injenious   ingenious

injer   injure

injery   injury

injure [injuring injured]

injury   injuries
injustice
ink   inky
inkling
inklude   include

Check out
inc as well

inkrease   increase
inkredibul   incredible
inkurabul   incurable
inkwest   inquest
inland
in-laws
inlay   inlaid
inlet
inlore   in-law
inmate
inn *[pub]*   in *[go in]*
innability   inability
innaccurate   inaccurate
innedibul   inedible
inner   innermost
innevitabul   inevitable
innings
innocence
innocent   innocently
innoculate   inoculate

innosent   innocent
innovation
innumerable
innundate   inundate
inocent   innocent
inoculate   inoculation
    [inoculating inoculated]
inoffensive
inokulate   inoculate
inormity   enormity
inormous   enormous
input [inputting input]
inquest
inquire   inquiry
inquisitive   inquisitively
inquisitiveness
insane   insanely
insanity
inscription
insect
insecure   insecurely
insecurity   insecurities
insekt   insect
insekure   insecure
insensitive   insensitively
insensitivity
insentiv   incentive
inseparable

insert   insertion

[inserting inserted]

insessant   incessant

inside

insidens   incidents

insident   incident

insight   incite *[stir up]

*[understanding]

insignificance

insignificant   insignificantly

insincere   insincerely

insincerity

insipid   insipidness

insishun   incision

insist insistent [insisting insisted]

insistence   insistently

insite   incite *[stir up]

                insight

                *[understanding]

insolant   insolent

insolence

insolent   insolently

insomnia   insomniac

insomya   insomnia

inspect inspection inspector

[inspecting inspected]

inspekt   inspect

inspektor   inspector

inspire   inspiration

[inspiring inspired]

install [installing installed]

instalment

instance   instants

     *[example]   *[moments]

instant   instantly

instead

instinct

institushun   institution

institute

institution   institutional

instorl   install

instrement   instrument

instruct [instructing instructed]

instruction   instructor

instrukt   instruct

instrument   instrumental

insufficient   insufficiently

insufishent   insufficient

insulate   insulation

[insulating insulated]

insulayt   insulate

insulin

insult [insulting insulted]

insurance

insure *[cover]   ensure *[be sure]

[insuring insured]

insurt   insert

intact

intake

intakt   intact

inteereer   interior

integrait   integrate

integrate integration
  [integrating integrated]

integrity

intelecchual   intellectual

inteligense   intelligence

inteligent   intelligent

intellectual intellectually

intelligence

intelligent intelligently

intend [intending intended]

intense intensely

intenshun   intention

intenshunal   intentional

intensity

intensive intensively

intention intentional

intentionally

interact interaction
  [interacting interacted]

interactive

interagayshun interrogation

interest [interesting interested]

interface

interfere interference
  [interfering interfered]

interior

interminable interminably

intermission

intermittent intermittently

internal internally

internashunal international

international internationally

Internet

interogate   interrogate

interpret interpretation
  [interpreting interpreted]

interrogate [interrogated]

interrogation

interrupt interruption
  [interrupting interrupted]

intersect intersection
  [intersecting intersected]

intersperse [interspersed]

interval

intervene intervention
  [intervening intervened]

interview
  [interviewing interviewed]

intervue   interview

interweave [interwoven]

intestine

intimait   intimate

intimate   intimately

intimidate   intimidation

   [intimidating intimidated]

intirier   interior

into

intolerable   intolerably

intolerance   intolerant

intolrabul   intolerable

intolrance   intolerance

intoxicated   intoxication

intreeg   intrigue

intrepid   intrepidly

intrest   interest

intricate   intricately

intrigue [intriguing intrigued]

intrikit   intricate

introduce

  [introducing introduced]

introduction   introductory

introjuce   introduce

introod   intrude

introoshun   intrusion

introvert   introverted

intrude [intruding intruded]

intrushun   intrusion

intrusion   intrusive

intuishun   intuition

intuition

inturest   interest

Check out
inter as well

inturfeer   interfere

inturmishun   intermission

inturnal   internal

Inturnet   Internet

inturpret   interpret

inturvue   interview

intwinded   entwined

Inuit

inumerabul   innumerable

invade [invading invaded]

invalid

invaluable

invashun   invasion

invasion

invayd   invade

invent   invention   inventor

  [inventing invented]

inventive   inventiveness

invertebrate

invert [inverted]

invest investment investor

  [investing invested]

investigate   investigation
[investigating investigated]

investigator

invirtibrate   invertebrate

invisibility

invisible   invisibly

invite   invitation
[inviting invited]

involuntary   involuntarily

involuntry   involuntary

involve [involving involved]

involvement

invurtebrate   invertebrate

inward   inwardly   inwards

inwud   inward

iradicate   eradicate

irase   erase

irate   irately

irational   irrational

Check out
irr as well

iregular   irregular

irelevent   irrelevant

ireplaceabul   irreplaceable

iresistibul   irresistible

iresponsibul   irresponsible

ireversibul   irreversible

irigate   irrigate

Irish

iritabul   irritable

iritate   irritate

irly   early

irn   earn *[money]
          urn *[vase]

irnest   earnest

irning   ironing

iron [ironing ironed]

ironic   ironically

ironik   ironic

ironmongers

irony

irrashunal   irrational

irrate   irate

irrational   irrationally

irregular   irregularly

irregularity   irregularities

irrelevant   irrelevance

irresistible   irresistibly

irresponsible   irresponsibly

irreverent   irreverently

irreversible

irrigate   irrigation
[irrigating irrigated]

irritability

irritable   irritably

115

irritate   irritation

  [irritating irritated]

irth   earth

ise   ice *[cold]

            eyes *[see]

ishue   issue

isicul   icicle

ising   icing

Islam   Islamic

island   islander

isle *[island]   aisle *[passage]

isn't [is not]

isolashun   isolation

isolate [isolating isolated]

isolation

isosceles triangle

isosulees   isosceles

issue [issuing issued]

isue   issue

it

italics

itch [itching itched]

itchy

item

iternal   eternal

iternity   eternity

ither   either

it'll [it will, shall]

its *[belongs]   it's *[it is, has]

itself

iturnity   eternity

ivacuate   evacuate

ivaluate   evaluate

ivaporate   evaporate

I've [I have]

ivolve   evolve

ivory

ivry   ivory

ivy

iye   I *[me]

            eye *[see]

iznt   isn't [is not]

jab [jabbing jabbed]

jack ~daw ~knife ~pot

jackal

jacket

jagged

jaguar

jail [jailing jailed] jailer

jak   jack

jaket   jacket

jale   jail

jam [jamming jammed]

Janery   January

jangle [jangling jangled]

January

Janyorary   January

jar [jarring jarred]

jargon

javelin

jaw jawbone

jazz jazzy

jealous jealously jealousy

Check out ge as well

jeans *[denim]   genes *[DNA]

jeer [jeering jeered]

jelisy   jealousy

jelly jellies jellied

jellyfish

jelus   jealous

jentil   gentle

jeriatric   geriatric

jerk [jerking jerked]

jerky jerkier jerkiest

jernal   journal

jerney   journey

jersey

jest [jesting jested] jester

Jesus Christ

jet [jetting jetted]

jet-propelled

jetty jetties

Jew *[religion]   dew *[drops]
                   due *[owing]

jewel *[gem]   dual *[two]
                duel *[fight]

jewelled

jeweller jewellery

Jewish

jewn   June

jier   jeer

jig [jigging jigged]

jiggle [jiggling jiggled]

jigsaw

jilt [jilted]

jingle [jingling jingled]

jirarf   giraffe
jittery
Jluy   July
job   jobless
jockey   jockeys
jodhpurs
jog [jogging jogged]
join [joining joined]   joiner
joint   jointly
joke [joking joked] joker
jokingly
jolly   jollier   jolliest
jolt [jolting jolted]
joos   deuce *[card]
                juice *[drink]
josel   jostle
jostle [jostling jostled]
jot [jotting jotted]
journal   journalism
journalist
journey
   [journeys journeying journeyed]
joust [jousting jousted]
jowst   joust
joy   joyful   joyfully
joyn   join
joynt   joint
joyride [joyriding]

jubilant
jubilee
judge [judging judged]
judgement
judo
juel   duel
jug
juggernaut
juggle [juggling juggled]
juggler
juice *[drink]   deuce *[card]
juicy   juicier   juiciest
jujitsu
July
jumble [jumbling jumbled]
jumbo jet
jump [jumping jumped]
jumper
jumpy   jumpier   jumpiest
juncshun   junction
junction
June *[month]   dune *[sand]
jungle   jungly
junior
junk
junkshun   junction
junyer   junior
Jupiter

jurnal	journal	justification	
jurney	journey	justify [justifies justifying justified]	
juror		justiss	justice
jursey	jersey	jut [jutting jutted]	
jury juries		juvenile	
juse	juice *[drink]	juwel	jewel *[gem]
	Jews *[people]	Juze	Jews *[people]
just justly			juice *[drink]
justice			

kab	cab		kave	cave
kabbige	cabbage		kayak [kayaking]	
kafé	café		keal	keel
kage	cage		kean	keen
kaki	khaki		keap	keep
kalculate	calculate		kebab	
kalculater	calculator		kechup	ketchup
kaleidoscope			kee	key *[lock]
kalender	calendar			quay *[dock]
kalidoscope	kaleidoscope		keel [keeling keeled]	
kame	came		keen keenly keenness	
kamp	camp		keep keeper keepsake	
kan	can		[keeping kept]	
kangaroo kangaroos			keesh	quiche
kanoo	canoe		keg	
kapchur	capture		kelidoscope	kaleidoscope
karatee	karate		kemist	chemist
karaoke			kennel	
karate			kept	
kareer	career *[job]		kerb *[edge]	curb *[stop]
karet	carat *[gold]		kernel *[seed]	colonel *[army]
	carrot *[veg]		kestrel	
karioke	karaoke		ketchup	
karki	khaki		kettle kettledrum	
karnival	carnival		key *[lock]	quay *[dock]
kart [karting]			keyboard keyhole keypad	
kasett	cassette		khaki	
kaution	caution		kibab	kebab

kic   kick

kichen   kitchen

kick [kicking kicked]

kick-off kick-start

kid   [kidding kidded]

kidnap kidnapper
  [kidnapping kidnapped]

kidney kidneys

kight   kite

kik   kick

kill [killing killed]

killd   killed

killer

kiln

kilo ~byte ~gram

kilo ~metre ~watt

kilt [kilted]

kind kindly kindness

kindergarten

kind-hearted

king kingdom

kingfisher

king-size king-sized

kiosk

kipper

kirb   curb *[stop]
     kerb *[edge]

kiss [kisses kissing kissed]

kit *[gear]   kite *[sky]

kitchen

kite

kitten

kiwi

Kleenex™

kleptomania kleptomaniac

klorafill   chlorophyll

knack

knackered

knave *[Jack] nave *[church]

knead *[dough] kneed *[knee]
     need *[must have]

knee [knees kneeing kneed]

kneed *[knee] knead *[dough]
     need *[have to]

kneel [kneeling knelt]

knew *[fact] new *[not old]

knickers

knick-knack

knife knives
  [knifes knifing knifed]

knight *[sir] night *[dark]

knit *[needles] nit *[hair]
     night *[dark]

knob knobbly knobblier

knock [knocking knocked]

knock-kneed

knollage   knowledge

knot *[tie]   not *[no]

knotty

know *[fact]   no *[not]

know [knowing knew known]

knowingly

knowledge   knowledgeable

knowledgeably

known

knuckle   knuckles

  [knuckling knuckled]

koala bear

kollekshun   collection

Koran

kore   core *[centre]

          corps *[army]

korgi   corgi

koridor   corridor

korps   corpse

kort   caught *[ball]

          court *[law]

Kouran   Koran

krate   crate

krater   crater

krave   crave

krew   crew

krews   crews *[teams]

          cruise *[trip]

krismus   Christmas

Check out ch as well

kung fu

kurb   curb *[stop]

          kerb *[edge]

kurnel   kernel *[seed]

          colonel *[army]

kwack   quack

kwestshun   question

kwestshunaire   questionnaire

kwick   quick

kwiert   quiet

Check out qu as well

L-plate

labals   labels

label

laber   labour

laboratory   laboratories

laborious   laboriously

labour [labouring laboured]

labourer

Labour Party

Labrador

lace   [lacing laced]   lacy

lack [lacking lacked]

lacquer

lacrosse

lad

ladder

laden

ladle [ladling ladled]

lady   ladies

ladybird

laff   laugh

lag [lagging lagged]

lager *[beer]   larger *[size]

laid

lain *[down]   lane *[path]

lair *[den]   layer *[cover]

lak   lack

lake   lakeside

laker   lacquer

lakross   lacrosse

lamb

lame   lamely   lameness

lament [lamenting lamented]

lamp   lampshade

land [landing landed]

land   ~lady ~lord ~mark

land   ~mine ~slide

Land Rover™

landscape [landscaping landscaped]

lane *[path]   lain *[down]

language

langwij   language

lanky   lankier   lankiest

lantern

lap [lapping lapped]

lapel

lapse [lapsing lapsed]

laptop

larder

larf   laugh

large   largely   largeness

larger *[bigger]   lager *[beer]

largest

larj   large

lark [larking larked]

larva *[insect]   lava *[rock]

larvae

lase   lace *[shoes]

                        laze *[relax]

laser

lash [lashing lashed]

lash   lashes

lass   lassie   lasses

lasso lassos

last [lasting lasted]

lastly

lasue   lasso

latch [latches latched]

late   lately   lateness

latecomer

later *[after]   latter *[last]

latest

Latin

latitude

latter *[last]   later *[after]

latter   latterly

lauf   laugh

laugh [laughing laughed]

laughable   laughingly

laught   laughed

laughter

launch

   [launches launching launched]

launder [laundered]

launderette   laundry

lava *[rock]   larva *[insect]

lavatory   lavatories

lavender

law   lawyer

lawful   lawfully

lawless   lawlessness

lawn   lawnmower

lay [laying laid]

lay   ~about ~man ~out

layer *[cover]   lair *[den]

laze *[relax]   lace *[shoes]

laze [lazing lazed]

lazer   laser

lazy   lazier   laziest

lead *[metal]   led *[took]

lead   leaded   leaden

lead [leading led]

leader   leadership

leaf   leaves   leafy

leaflet

league

leaisure   leisure

leak *[hole]   leek *[veg]

   [leaking leaked]

leakage

leaky   leakier leakiest

lean [leaning leaned leant]

lean leaner leanest

leant *[past of lean]

lent *[past of lend]
Lent *[before Easter]

leap [leaping leapt leaped]

leapfrog

learn [learning learnt learned]

lease [leasing leased]

least

leather leathery

leave [leaving left]

leaves

leccher   lecture

lectern

lecture [lecturing lectured]

lecturn   lectern

led *[guided]   lead *[metal]

leding   leading

ledge

lee ~ward ~way

Leebra   Libra

leece   lease

leech leeches

leed   lead

leef   leaf

leeg   league

leek *[veg]   leak *[hole]

leer [leering leered]

left left-handed

leftenant   lieutenant

leftovers

leg [legging legged]

legal legally

legalise [legalising legalised]

legend legendary

legibility legibly

legible

legislation

legitimate legitimately

leisure leisurely

lej   ledge

lejion   legion

lemon lemonade

lend [lending lent] lender

lene   lean

length ~ways ~wise

lengthen [lengthening lengthened]

lengthy lengthier lengthiest

lenient leniently

lens lenses

lent *[past of lend]

Lent   leant
*[before Easter]   *[past of lean]

lentil

Leo

leopard

leotard

lepard   leopard

leper leprosy

lept   leapt

lerch   lurch

lerk   lurk

lern   learn

lesher   leisure

less lesser least

lessen *[reduce] [lessening lessened]

lesson *[class]

let [letting let]

lethal lethally

lethargic

lether   leather

letiss   lettuce

letter lettering

lettuce

leukaemia

level [levelling levelled]

lever

liable

liaise [liaising liaised]

liaison

liar *[lies]   lyre *[music]

liase   liaise

libel

liberal liberally

Liberal Democrat Party

liberate [liberating liberated]

liberty liberties

Libra

libral   liberal

librarian

library libraries

librury   library

lice

licence *[document]

license *[allow] [licensing licensed]

lichen

lick [licking licked]

licker   liquor

lickoriss   liquorice

lid lidded

lide   lied

lie [lies lying lied]

liebraree   library

lier   leer

lieutenant

life lives

life ~belt ~boat ~buoy

life ~less ~like ~line ~long

life ~span ~style ~time

life-threatening

lift [lifting lifted]

light [lighting lit]

light   ~house ~weight

light   lighter   lightest

lighten [lightening lightened]

lightening *[make lighter]

lightly   lightness

lightning *[flash]

liing   lying

like [liking liked]

likeable

likely   likeness

liken [likening likened]

likewise

likwid   liquid

lilac

lily   lilies

limb [limbed]

lime   ~light ~stone

limerick

limit [limiting limited]

limitation

limitless

limousine

limozeen   limousine

limp [limping limped]

limpet

linch   lynch

line [lining lined]

linear

linen

linesman

linger [lingering lingered]

linguist

lining

link [linking linked]

links *[joins]   lynx *[animal]

linoleum   lino

lion   lioness   lionesses

lip   lip-read

lipstick

liquid

liquidise   liquidiser
  [liquidising liquidised]

liquor

liquorice

lirch   lurch

lire   liar *[tells lies]
                  lyre *[music]

liric   lyric

lisen   listen

lisence   licence
                      *[document]
                  license *[allow]

lison   listen

lisp [lisping lisped]

lissen   listen

list

listen [listening listened]

litel — little

liten — lighten

literacy — literate

literal — literally

literature

litewait — lightweight

litly — lightly

litning — lightning

litrcy — literacy

litre *[measurement]

litter *[rubbish] [littering littered]

little littler littlest

littrit — literate

live [living lived]

livelihood

lively livelier liveliest

liver

livestock

livid

lizard

llama

load [loading loaded]

loaf *[bread] loaves

loaf *[laze] [loafing loafed]

loan *[lend] lone *[alone]

[loaning loaned]

loathe [loathing loathed]

loathsome

lob [lobbing lobbed]

lobster

local locally

locality localities

locamotiv — locomotive

locate [located] location

loch *[lake]

Loch Ness Monster

lock *[door, canal] [locking locked]

locket

locomotion locomotive

loct — locked

locust

lodge [lodging lodged]

lodgings

lods — loads

loft

loftier loftiest

log [logging logged]

loge — lodge

logic logical logically

logo logos

loiter [loitering loitered]

lojic — logic

lok — loch *[lake]

lock *[door]

lokal   local

lokalitee   locality

lokate   locate

lokomoshun   locomotion

lokust   locust

loll [lolling lolled]

lollipop   lolly   lollies

lone *[alone]   loan *[lend]

lonely   lonelier   loneliest

loner

long [longing longed]

longer   longest

longingly

longitude

look [looking looked]

look   ~alike ~out

loom [looming loomed]

loonatic   lunatic

loop [looping looped]

loophole

loose *[not tight]   lose *[not win]

loose   looser   loosest

loosely   looseness

loosen [loosening loosened]

loot *[goods]   lute *[musical]
   [looting looted]

lopsided

lord   lordly

Lords [the]

loreful   lawful

lorless   lawless

lornch   launch

lorndree   laundry

lornmower   lawnmower

lorry   lorries

lose *[not win] loose *[not tight]
   [losing lost]

loshun   lotion

loss   losses

lost

lot

lotion

lottery   lotteries

lotto

lottree   lottery

loud   louder   loudest

loudly   loudness

loud   ~mouth ~speaker

lounge [lounging lounged]

lousy   lousier   lousiest

lout   loutish

lovable

love [loving loved]   lover

love   ~sick ~song

lovely   lovelier   loveliest

loving   lovingly

low   lower   lowest

low   ~lands ~ness

lowd   loud

lower [lowering lowered]

lowly   lowlier   lowliest

lownge   lounge

lowsy   lousy

lowt   lout

loyal   loyally

loyalty   loyalties

loyer   lawyer

loyter   loiter

lozenge

lrst   last

luck lucky luckier luckiest

lucksurius   luxurious

lucksury   luxury

lucly   luckily

ludicrous   ludicrously

lug [lugging lugged]

luggage

luggige   luggage

lukeemia   leukaemia

lukewarm

lull [lulling lulled]

lullaby   lullabies

lumber [lumbering lumbered]

lumberjack

lume   loom

luminous

lump [lumping lumped]

lumpy   lumpier   lumpiest

lunacy   lunatic

lunar

lunasy   lunacy

lunch   lunches

lunchtime

luner   lunar

lung

lunge [lunging lunged]

lurch [lurches lurching lurched]

lure [luring lured]

lurk [lurking lurked]

lurn   learn

luscious

luse   loose *[not tight]

                  lose *[not win]

lush   lusher   lushest

lushus   luscious

lusse   loose

lussen   loosen

lust   lustful   lustfully

lute *[music]   loot *[goods]

luvly   lovely

luxurious   luxuriously

luxury   luxuries

ly	lie

Check out
li as well

lyase	liaise
lybraree	library
lyce	lice
Lycra™	

lyer	liar *[tells lies]
	lyre *[music]
lying	
lynch [lynching lynched]	
lyon	lion
lyre *[music]	liar *[lies]
lyrics lyrical	

ma'am

macaroni

macaw

Mach   March

mach   match

machete

machine   machinery

machine-gun

machure   mature

mack   make

mackerel

mackintosh   mackintoshes

macor   macaw

mad *[crazy]   made *[built]

           maid *[girl]

mad   madder   maddest

mad   madly   madness

madam

madden [maddening maddened]

made *[built]   mad *[crazy]

           maid *[girl]

maed   made

maer   mayor

maffs   maths

magazine

mager   major

magestic   majestic

magesty   majesty

maggot

magic   magical   magically

magician

magistrate

magnesium

magnet   magnetic

magnificent   magificently

magnify

   [magnifies magnifying magnified]

magnification

magnifying glass

magots   maggots

magpie

mahogany

maid *[girl]   made *[built, did]

mail *[post]   male *[man]

   [mailing mailed]

maim [maiming maimed]

main *[chief]   mane *[hair]

mainly

maintain [maintaining maintained]

maintenance

mait   mate

maize *[corn]   maze *[lost]

majestic   majestically

majesty   majesties

majic   magic

majishun   magician

majistrate   magistrate

major

majority

mak   make

makaroni   macaroni

make [making made] maker

make-believe

making

makintosh   mackintosh

maksimum   maximum

malaria

male *[man]   mail *[post]

malicious   maliciously

mall *[shops]   maul *[hurt]

mallet

malnewtrishun malnutrition

malnutrition

mame   maim

mammal

mammoth

man [manning manned]

man   ~eater ~kind ~power

manage   manageable

  [managing managed]

management

manager *[boss] manger *[box]

mandarin

mane *[hair]   main *[chief]

maner   manner

manewer   manure

mange   mangy

manged   managed

manger *[box]   manager *[boss]

mangle [mangled]

mango   mangoes

manhandle

  [manhandling manhandled]

mania

maniac *[mad person]

manic *[excited]

manicure

manipulate

  [manipulating manipulated]

manipulative

maniqure   manicure

manly   manlier   manliest

manliness

manner *[way]   manor *[house]

manners

manor *[house]   manner *[way]

manshun   mansion

mansion

manslaughter

manslorter   manslaughter

mantelpiece

manual   manually

manufacture [manufactured]

manufacturer

manure

manuscript

many   more   most

Maori

map [mapping mapped]

marathon

marble

march *[walk] marches
[marching marched]

March *[month]

mare *[horse]   mayor *[city]

margarine

margin

marige   marriage

marigold

marina *[harbour]

marine *[army, sea]

marjarin   margarine

marjin   margin

mark [marking marked]

marker

market [marketing marked]

markey   marquee

marksman

marmalade

maroon [marooned]

marquee

marreid   married

marriage

marrow

marry [marries marrying married]

Mars   Martian

marsh   marshy

Marshan   Martian

marshine   machine

marshmallow

marsipan   marzipan

marst   mast

martial arts

Martian

martyr   martyrdom

marune   maroon

marvel [marvelling marvelled]

marvellous   marvellously

marys   marries

marzipan

masaker   massacre

masarge   massage

mascara

mascot

masculine

mash [mashes mashing mashed]

mashetee   machete

mashine   machine

mask *[cover]   masque *[ball]
  [masking masked]
maskot   mascot
maskulin   masculine
mass   masses
massacre [massacring massacred]
massage [massaging massaged]
massive   massively
mast
master [mastering mastered]
master   ~mind ~piece
masterful   masterfully
mastermind [masterminded]
mat *[rug]   mate *[friend]
                matt *[dull]
matador
match   matches
  [matching matched]
match   ~box ~less ~maker
mate [mating mated]
matedor   matador
material   materialistic
maternal   maternally
maternity
mathematician
mathematics   mathematical
maths
matinée

matiriel   material
matrimony
matrix   matrices
matron   matronly
matt *[dull]   mat *[rug]
matter [mattered]
matting
mattress   mattresses
mature   maturely   maturity
  [maturing matured]
maturnal   maternal
maul *[hurt]   mall *[shops]
  [mauling mauled]
mauve
maveles   marvellous
maximum
may *[perhaps]   May *[month]
maybe
mayday *[SOS]   May Day
                *[1st May]
mayde   made *[built]
                maid *[girl]
maym   maim
mayonnaise
mayor *[city]   mare *[horse]
mayoress
mayt   mate
maze *[lost]   maize *[corn]

135

me
meadow
meal ~time
mean *[average, imply]
  [meaning meant]
mean meaner meanest
mean *[nasty]
meaning ~ful ~fully ~less
meanly meanness
meant
meantime
meanwhile
measles
measurable
measure measurement
  [measuring measured]
meat *[flesh]   meet *[hello]
meaty meatier meatiest
mecanic   mechanic
Mecca
mechanic mechanical
mechanically
mechanism
medal *[award]   meddle *[pry]
medallion
medallist
meddle *[pry]   medal *[award]
  [meddling meddled]

meddow   meadow
media
median
medical medically
medication
medicine medicinal
medieval
meditate meditation
  [meditating meditated]
Mediterranean
medium
meek meeker meekest
meekly
meet *[hello]   meat *[flesh]
  [meeting met]
mega ~byte ~phone
megafone   megaphone
Meka   Mecca
mekanic   mechanic
melen   melon
melon
melt [melting melted]
member ~ship
Member of Parliament
membrane
memo
memoirs
memorable memorably

memorial	mersiless **merciless**
memorise [memorising memorised]	mesels **measles**
memory memories	mesh [meshes meshed]
men	meshurabul **measurable**
menace [menacing menaced]	meshure **measure**
menay **many**	mesige **message**
mend [mending mended]	mess [messing messed]
meniss **menace**	message messaging
menshun **mention**	messenger
mental mentally	messtak **mistake**
mentality	messy messier messiest
mention [mentioning mentioned]	met
menu menus	metafor **metaphor**
meny **many**	metal metallic
merang **meringue**	metaphor
merchant	meteor meteorite
merciful mercifully	meter *[gas] metre *[length]
merciless mercilessly	method
mercury *[metal]	methodical methodically
Mercury *[planet]	methylated spirits meths
mercy mercies	metior **meteor**
merder **murder**	metre *[length] meter *[gas]
merge [merging merged]	metric
meringue	mew [mewing mewed]
merit [meriting merited]	mewchal **mutual**
mermaid	mewseum **museum**
mermer **murmur**	mewsik **music**
merry merrier merriest	mewsishan **musician**

mewtinear mutineer	mikroskope microscope
Mey May	mild milder mildest
miaow [miaowing miaowed]	mildew
mice	mildly mildness
micro ~chip ~light	mile mileage milestone
micro ~phone ~scope	military
micro ~scopic ~wave	milk [milking milked]
midday midnight	milk ~man ~shake
middle	milky milkier milkiest
Middle East	Milky Way
midge	mill [milling milled] miller
midget	millennium
midia media	milligram millilitre
midian median	millimetre
midium medium	million ~aire ~airess
midst *[middle] mist *[fog]	millionth
missed *[let go]	millipede
midul middle	mime [miming mimed]
midwife midwives	mimic [mimicking mimicked]
miget midget	mince
might mite *[insect]	mind [minding minded]
*[strength, may]	mindless mindlessly
mighty mightier mightiest	mine [mining mined]
migraine	mine ~field ~sweeper
migrate migration	miner *[coal] minor *[lesser]
[migrating migrated]	mineral
migt might	minet minute
mike	mingle [mingling mingled]

138

mini ~beast ~bus ~skirt

miniature

minimum

minister

ministry   ministries

mink

minnow

minor *[lesser]   miner *[coal]

minority

minstrel

mint

minus

minut   minute

minute *[time]

minute *[small]   minutely

miracle

miraculous   miraculously

mirage

mirarj   mirage

mirge   merge

mirmade   mermaid

mirmer   murmur

mirror

misbehave   misbehaviour
  [misbehaving misbehaved]

miscarriage

miscellaneous

mischief   mischievous

mise   mice

miser   miserly

miserable   miserably

misery   miseries

misfire [misfiring misfired]

misfit

misfortune

misgide   misguide

misgivings

misheard

mishun   mission

misjudge [misjudging misjudged]

mislay [mislaying mislaid]

mislead [misleading misled]

misplace [misplaced]

misprint

misrabull   miserable

miss [missing missed]

missed *[failed]   mist *[fog]

missile

missing

mission

missionary   missionaries

misspell [misspelling misspelt]

mist *[fog]   missed *[failed]

mistake
  [mistaking mistook mistaken]

misterius   mysterious

139

Check out
my as well

mistic	**mystic**
mistifyed	**mystified**
mistletoe	
mistook	
mistreat mistreatment	
[mistreating mistreated]	
mistress mistresses	
mistrust [mistrusted]	
mistry	**mystery**
misty mistier mistiest	
misunderstand	
[misunderstanding misunderstood]	
misuse [misusing misused]	
mite *[insect]	**might** *[strength, may]
mith	**myth**
mity	**mighty**
mix [mixing mixed] mixture	
miy	**my**
mizer	**miser**
mizeree	**misery**
mizrabul	**miserable**
mnemonic	
moan *[groan]	mown *[grass]
moat	

mob [mobbing mobbed]
mobile phone
mobility
mock [mocking mocked]
mockery
mode
model [modelling modelled]
modem
moderate moderately
modern
modernise modernisation
 [modernising modernised]
modest modestly modesty
modurn   **modern**
moist moisture
moisten [moistening moistened]
molar
molde   **mould**
mole molehill
molecule molecular
molte   **moult**
molten
moment momentous
momentum
monaky   **monarchy**
monarch
monarchy monarchies
monastery monastries

monastic

Monday

money [moneyed]

mongoose

mongrel

monie   money

monitor [monitoring monitored]

monk

monkey

monologue

monopolise

  [monopolising monopolised]

monopoly

monotonous   monotony

monotonously

monsieur

monsoon

monster   monstrous

monstrosity   monstrosities

monsyer   monsieur

month   monthly

monument   monumental

mony   money

moo [mooing mooed]

mood *[temper]   mooed *[cow]

moody   moodier   moodiest

moon   ~beam ~light

moon   ~lit ~shine

moor *[land]   more *[greater]

moor *[boat] [mooring moored]

moorhen

moose *[deer]   mousse *[pud]

mooslee   muesli

moove   move

moovee   movie

mop *[clean] [mopping mopped]

mope *[do nothing] [moping moped]

moped *[bike]

mopped *[cleaned]

moral *[good] morally

morale *[confidence]

morality

morbid   morbidly

more *[greater]   moor *[land]

moreover

morgige   mortgage

morl   maul *[hurt]

       mall *[shops]

mornful   mournful

morning

Morse code

morsel

mortal   mortality

mortally

mortar

mortgage [mortgaged]

mortuary

mosaic

moshun   motion

mosk   mosque

moskito   mosquito

mosque

mosquito   mosquitoes

moss   mosses   mossy

most   mostly

motel

moth   motheaten

mother   motherhood

motherly

motion   motionless

motivate   motivator
 [motivating motivated]

motivation

motive

motor [motoring motored]

motor   ~bike ~boat

motor   ~cycle ~cyclist

motor   ~ist ~way

motorised

motto   mottoes

mould [moulding moulded]

mouldy   mouldier   mouldiest

moult [moulting moulted]

mound

mount [mounting mounted]

mountain   mountainous

mountaineer   mountaineering

mourn *[sad]   morn *[a.m.]
 [mourning mourned]

mournful   mournfully

mouse   mice

mousse *[pud]   moose *[deer]

moustache

mousy

mouth   mouthful

move [moving moved]

movement

mow [mowing mowed mown]

mower

mown *[grass]   moan *[groan]

mownd   mound

mowntain   mountain

Mowri   Maori

mowse   mouse

mowth   mouth

moyst   moist

much

muck [mucking mucked]

mucky   muckier   muckiest

mud

muddle [muddling muddled]

muddy   muddier   muddiest

muing	mewing
muel	mule
muesli	
muffin	
muffle [muffling muffled]	
mug [mugging mugged]	
mule	
multicoloured	
multicultural	
multilingual	
multi-millionaire	
multiple	
multiplication	
multiply [multiplies]	
[multiplying multiplied]	
multiracial	
multi-storey	
mum	
mumble [mumbling mumbled]	
mummy mummies	
mumps	
munch [munching munched]	
munches	
Mundy	Monday
mune	moon
muney	money
mungrel	mongrel
munk	monk

munkey	monkey
munsh	munch
muny	money
mural	
murang	meringue
murcy	mercy
murder [murdering murdered]	
murderer murderess	
murderous	
murge	merge
murky murkier murkiest	
murmaid	mermaid
murmur [murmuring murmured]	
mursee	mercy
mursiful	merciful
muscle *[body] mussel *[eat]	
[muscling muscled]	
muscular	
museum	
mushy	
mushroom	
music musical musically	
musician	
musik	music
musishan	musician
musium	museum
musket musketeer	
Muslim	

143

mussel *[eat]   muscle *[body]

must   mustn't [must not]

mustard

mustash   moustache

musty   mustier   mustiest

mutant

mute [muted]

mutineer

mutiny   mutinies

mutter [muttering muttered]

muvabul   movable

muve   move

muzzle [muzzling muzzled]

my   myself

myaow   miaow

Check out
mi as well

myld   mild

mynah *[bird]   minor *[lesser]

mysterious   mysteriously

mystery   mysteries

mystify [mystifies]

  [mystifying mystified]

myth   mythical

nacher   nature
nacheral   natural
nag [nagging nagged]
nail [nailing nailed]
nail-biting
nak   knack
naked   nakedness
nale   nail
name [naming named]
nameless   namely
nanny   nannies
nap [napping napped]
napkin
nappy   nappies
narled   gnarled
narrate   narrator
  [narrating narrated]
narration   narrative
narrow   narrower   narrowest
narrowly
narrow-minded
nasal
nash   gnash
nashun   nation
nashunality   nationality
nasty   nastier   nastiest
nat   gnat
nation   nationwide

national
National Health Service
nationality   nationalities
native
Nativity
natural   naturally
naturalist
nature
naughtier   naughtiest
naughty
nausea   nauseous
naval *[navy]   navel *[tummy]
navee   navy
navel *[tummy]   naval *[navy]
navey   navy
navigate   navigator
  [navigating navigated]
navigation
navul   naval *[navy]
              navel *[tummy]
navy   navies
naw   gnaw *[bite]
              nor *[neither]
nawr   now
naybor   neighbour
naytiv   native
nazel   nasal
Nazi   Nazism

nead   knead *[dough]

need *[must have]

kneed *[with
knee]

neadle   needle

near   nearer   nearest

near   nearby   nearly

neat   neater   neatest

neatly   neatness

necessarily

necessary

neck   necklace

necst   next

nectar   nectarine

nee   knee

need *[must have] knead *[dough]

needle [needling needled]

needless   needlessly

needy   needier   neediest

neel   kneel

neer   near

neese   niece

nefew   nephew

negative   negatively

neglect   neglectful
[neglecting neglected]

negotiate [negotiating negotiated]

neigh [neighing neighed]

neighbour   neighbouring

neighbourhood   neighbourly

neither

nek   neck

nekst   next

nelt   knelt

nemonic   mnemonic

neon

nephew

nerse   nurse

nerve   nerve-racking

nervous   nervously

nervousness   nervy

nesessary   necessary

nest [nesting nested]

nestle [nestling nestled]

net *[mesh]   neat *[tidy]

net   netball   network

netley   neatly

nettle

neuter [neutered]

neutral

never   nevertheless

new *[not old]   knew *[fact]

newer   newest

newly   newness

new   ~born   ~comer

newclear   nuclear

newcleus	nucleus

Check out
nu as well

newdist	nudist
newgar	nougat
newmerus	numerous
news	~agent ~flash
news	~letter ~paper ~reader
newsons	nuisance
newt	
newtrishun	nutrition
next	
nib	
nibble [nibbling nibbled]	
nice *[kind]	niece *[aunt]
nicer nicest nicely	
nick [nicking nicked]	
nickers	knickers
nickname [nicknamed]	
niece *[aunt]	nice *[kind]
nieghbour	neighbour
nier	near
niese	niece
niet	night
nife	knife
night *[dark]	knight *[man]
night	~club ~dress ~fall

night	~shirt ~time
nightingale	
nightly	
nightmare	nightmarish
nihgt	night
nikname	nickname
nil	
nilon	nylon
nimble nimbly	
nimf	nymph
nine ninth	
nineteen nineteenth	
ninety nineties ninetieth	
ninteen	nineteen
nip [nipping nipped]	
nipple	
nirve	nerve
nirvos	nervous
nise	nice *[kind]
nit *[insect]	knit *[wool]

Check out
kn as well

nite	knight *[man]
	night *[dark]
nither	neither
nitrogen	
nitting	knitting

no *[not]*   know *[fact]*

noble   nobleman   nobility

nobler   noblest   nobly

nobody

nock   knock

nocturnal

nod [nodding nodded]

noise   noiseless   noiselessly

noisy   noisier   noisiest

nollij   knowledge

nomad   nomadic

nome   gnome

noncense   nonsense

none *[not any]*   nun *[God]*

non-existent

non-fiction

nonsense

non-starter

non-stop

noodle

noon *[midday]*

no one *[not any person]*

noose

noospaper   newspaper

nor *[neither]*   gnaw *[bite]*

norghty   naughty

norm

normal   normality

normally

Norman Conquest

normly   normally

norsea   nausea

norseus   nauseous

north   ~bound   north-east

north   ~erly ~ern ~erner

North Pole

north   ~wards   north-west

norty   naughty

nose *[face]*   knows *[fact]*

nosedive [nosedived]

nostril

nosy   nosier   nosiest

not *[no]*   knot *[tie]*

notch   notches

note [noting noted]

note   ~book ~card

note   ~pad ~paper

nothing   nothingness

notice [noticing noticed]

noticeable   noticeably

noticeboard

notiss   notice

nought

noun *[word]*   known *[fact]*

nourish   nourishment

[nourishing nourished]

novel   novelist
novelty   novelties
November
now   nowadays
nowere   nowhere
nowhere
nowlege   knowledge
nown   known *[fact]
                noun *[word]
nowon   no one
noyse   noise
noze   knows *[fact]
                nose *[face]
nozzle
nuckel   knuckle
nuclear   nuclear power
nucleus   nuclei
nude   nudity
nudge [nudging nudged]
nue   knew *[fact]
                new *[not old]
nues   news
nugget
nuisance
nuj   nudge
numb   numbness

number [numbering numbered]
numeracy
numeral
numerasee   numeracy
numerator
numerical
numerous
numonia   pneumonia
nun *[God]   none *[not any]
nurrish   nourish
nurse [nursing nursed]
nursery   nurseries
nursing home
nurvous   nervous
nurvy   nervy
nut   nutcracker   nutshell
nute   newt
nuter   neuter
nutrition
nutron   neutron
nutty   nuttier   nuttiest
nuzzle [nuzzling nuzzled]
nxte   next
nylon
nymph

oad   ode *[poem]

owed *[money]

oaf oafish

oak

oan   own *[belongs]

oar   or *[alternative]

ore *[mineral]

oarsman

oasis oases

oath

obay   obey

obedient obedience

obediently

obedyans   obedience

obeece   obese

obese obesity

obey [obeying obeyed]

obidyant   obedient

object objector

[objecting objected]

objection objectionable

objective

objekt   object

obligation

oblige [obliging obliged]

oblong

oblyge   oblige

obnoxious

oboe oboist

obow   oboe

obscene obscenely

obscure obscurity

obseen   obscene

observant observation

observe observer

[observing observed]

obsessed obsession

obsessive

obskure   obscure

obsolete

obsqure   obscure

obsqurity   obscurity

obstacle

obstinacy

obstinate obstinately

obstruct obstruction

[obstructing obstructed]

obsurd   absurd

obsurve   observe

obtain obtainable

[obtaining obtained]

obtuse angle

obvious obviously

ocashun   occasion

occasional occasionally

occupation

occupy [occupies]
  [occupying occupied]
occur [occurring occurred]
ocean
ockur   occur
o'clock
octagon   octagonal
octave
octiv   octave
October
octopus   octopuses
ocupashun   occupation
ocupie   occupy
ocur   occur
odd   odder   oddest
oddity   oddities
oddly   oddments
ode *[poem]   owed *[money]
oder   odour
odour   odourless
ods   odds
of *[part]   off *[not on]
ofal   awful
of course
ofen   often
ofense   offence
ofensive   offensive
ofer   offer

off *[not on]   of *[part]
offence
offend [offending offended]
offensive   offensively
offer [offering offered]
offhand
office   officer
official   officially
officious   officiously
offside
offten   often
ofice   office
ofiser   officer
ofishall   official
ofsyd   offside
often
oger   ogre
ogre
Ogst   August
oh *[surprise]   owe *[money]
oil [oiling oiled]
oily   oilier   oiliest
ointment
okcupashun   occupation

Check out
oc as well

okcupyd   occupied

okcur	occur
o'klock	o'clock
oksidise	oxidise
oksygen	oxygen
oktagon	octagon
Oktober	October
oktopus	octopus
old	old-fashioned
Olimpic	Olympic
olive	
Olympic Games	
omelette	
omen	
ominous	ominously
omishun	omission
omission	
omit [omitting omitted]	
omlet	omelette
omminus	ominous
ommit	omit
omnivore	omnivorous
on	ongoing
once *[one time]	wants *[would like]
one *[single]	won *[victory]
one	one-way
oner	owner
onest	honest

onion	
online	
onlooker	
only	
onomatopoeia	onomatopoeic
onse	once
onset	
onslort	onslaught
onto	
onts	once
onward	onwards
onyun	onion
ooze [oozing oozed]	
opan	open
open [opening opened]	
openly	opener
opera	operatic
operashun	operation
operate	operator
[operating operated]	
opinion	opinionated
oponent	opponent
oposit	opposite
opponent	
opporchunity	opportunity
opportunity	opportunities
oppose [opposing opposed]	
opposite	opposition

oppress [oppresses]
  [oppressing oppressed]
oppression   oppressor
opra   opera
opropryet   appropriate
opshun   option
opt [opting opted]
optic optical
optician
optimism   optimistically
optimist   optimistic
option   optional
optishun   optician
opurate   operate
or *[either]   awe *[wonder]
                    oar *[boat]
                    ore *[mineral]
oral *[mouth]   aural *[ear]
orally
orange
orang-utan
orbit [orbiting orbited]
orchard
orchestra   orchestral
orchid
ordeal
order [ordering ordered]
orderly

ordinal number
ordinary   ordinarily
ordnary   ordinary
ordur   order
ore *[mineral]   awe *[wonder]
                    oar *[boat]
                    or *[either]
orfan   orphan
organ   organist
organic   organically
organise   organisation
  [organising organised]
organism
Orgust   August
oriant   orient
oriental
orienteering
origin
original   originally
originality
originate [originating originated]
orijin   origin
orijinal   original
oringe   orange
orkestra   orchestra
orl   all
ornament   ornamental
ornge   orange

orphan   orphanage   orphaned

ort   ought

orthodontist

ortistic   autistic

ortum   autumn

oshun   ocean

osmosis

Ostralyer   Australia

ostrich   ostriches

ote   oat

othar   other

otherwise

otter

ouch

ought *[should]

oughtn't *[should not]

oul   owl

ounce

our *[owns]   are *[we are]

                  hour *[time]

ourang-outang   orang-utan

ours *[owns]   hours *[time]

ourselves

out   ~back ~break

out   ~board ~burst ~come

out   ~door ~fit ~let ~line

out   ~look ~number ~patient

out   ~right ~set ~side ~skirts

outdo [outdoes]

  [outdoing outdid outdone]

outer space

outrayjus   outrageous

outrageous

outspoken

outstanding

outward   outwardly

outward-bound

outwards

owa   our

oval

ovary   ovaries

ovel   oval

oven   ovenproof

over   ~act ~arm ~board

over   ~cast ~coat ~come

over   ~do ~due ~flow

over   ~grown ~hang ~hear

over   ~heat ~joyed ~land

over   ~lap ~look ~seas

over   ~time ~weight

overtake [overtaking]

  [overtook overtaken]

overwait   overweight

overwelm   overwhelm

overwhelm [overwhelming]

  [overwhelmed]

ovursee	oversee
ow *[pain]	
owe *[money]	oh *[surprise]
[owing owed]	
owed *[money]	ode *[poem]
owl owlish	
own [owning owned]	
owner	
ownly	only
owtberst	outburst
owtdoor	outdoor

Check out
out as well

owter	outer
ox oxen oxtail	
oxygen	
oyel	oil
oyntment	ointment
oyster	
ozone layer	

pace [pacing paced]

pacemaker

pack [packing packed]

package

packed *[case]   pact *[deal]

packet

pact *[deal]   packed *[case]

pad *[cloth]   paid *[money]
  [padding padded]

paddle [paddling paddled]

paddock

pade   paid

padlock [padlocked]

pagan

page

paid

pain *[ow!]   pane *[glass]

pain ~free ~killer ~less

painful   painfully

paint [painting painted]

pair *[two]   pare *[trim]
                   pear *[fruit]

paj   page

paket   packet

palace   palatial

pale *[colour]   pail *[bucket]

paler   palest

paliss   palace

palm   palmist

Palm Sunday

pamflet   pamphlet

pamper [pampered]

pamphlet

pan   pancake

pane *[glass]   pain *[ow!]

panel

panic   panic-stricken

panicked   panicking   panicky

panorama   panoramic

pansy   pansies

pant [panting panted]

panther

pantomime

paper   ~back   ~work

papier-mâché

parachute [parachuting parachuted]

parade [parading paraded]

paradise

paragraph

parallel   parallelogram

paralyse [paralysed]

parashoot   parachute

parasite

parcel

parched

pardon [pardoned]

parellel	parallel	pasta	
parent		pastel	
park [parking parked]		pastime	
parlement	parliament	pastry pastries	
parliament		pat [patting patted]	
parm	palm	patch patches [patching patched]	
parrot		path	
parsel	parcel	pathetic pathetically	
parsley		patience *[calmness]	
parsnip		patients *[ill people]	
parst	past	patient patiently	
part [parting parted]		patio	
parth	path	patriotic	
partly		patrol [patrolling patrolled]	
partner		pattern [patterned]	
party parties		pause *[wait] paws *[feet]	
pashence	patience	[pausing paused]	
	*[calmness]	pave [paving paved]	
	patients	pavement	
	*[doctor's]	paw *[foot] poor *[needy]	
pashent	patient	[pawing pawed] pore *[skin, scan]	
pass [passing passed]			pour *[tip]
pass passport password		pawch	porch
passage passageway		paws *[feet]	pause *[stop]
passed *[over] past *[time]		pawshun	portion
passenger		pay [paying paid]	
passige	passage	payment	
past *[time]	passed *[over]	paynt	paint

pea

peace *[calm]   piece *[part]

peaceful   peacefully

peach   peaches

peacock

peak *[top]   peek *[glance]
   [peaking peaked]

peal *[bells]   peel *[skin]

peanut

pear *[fruit]   pare *[trim]

pearl *[gem]   purl *[knit]

pearly

peasant

pebble   pebbly

peculiar   peculiarity

pedal [pedalling pedalled]

pedestrian

peece   peace *[calm]
         piece *[part]

peech   peach

peek *[glance]   peak *[top]
   [peeking peeked]

peel *[skin]   peal *[bells]
   [peeling peeled]

peep [peeping peeped]

peer [peering peered]

peeriodd   period

peetza   pizza

peg [pegging pegged]

peice   peace *[calm]
         piece *[part]

pekuliar   peculiar

pelican   pelican crossing

pelt [pelting pelted]

pen

penalty   penalties

pence *[money]   pens *[ink]

pencil [pencilled]

penguin

pengwin   penguin

penicillin

peninsula

penisillin   penicillin

penknife   penknives

penniless

pens *[ink]   pence *[money]

penshun   pension

pensil   pencil

pension   pensioner

pentagon

pentathlon

people

peple   people

pepper   peppery

peppermint

pepule   people

per cent   percentage

perception   perceptive

perch [perches perching perched]

perchase   purchase

percussion

perfect [perfected]

perfection   perfectly

perform   performance
  [performing performed]

perfume

perhaps

perimeter

period

perish [perished]

perm [permed]

permanent   permanently

permission

permit [permitting permitted]

perpendicular

perple   purple

perposs   purpose

perr   purr

perse   purse

persecute [persecuting persecuted]

persenly   personally

persevere   perseverance
  [persevering persevered]

persist [persisted]

persistent   persistently

person   personal   personally

personality   personalities

persuade [persuading persuaded]

persuasion

persuasive

persue   pursue

persute   pursuit

perswade   persuade

pesant   peasant

pessimism

pessimist   pessimistic

pest   pesticide

pester [pestering pestered]

pet [petting petted]

petal

petishun   petition

petition

petrify [petrifies]
  [petrifying petrified]

petrol

petticoat

pew

pewpil   pupil

phantom

Pharaoh

phase

pheasant

phenomenal   phenomenon

phew *[sigh]   few *[not many]

philosopher

phoan   phone
*[telephone]

phobia

phone [phoning phoned]

phonics

photo   ~copier

photocopy [photocopied]

photograph [photographed]

photographer   photography

photosynthesis

phrase

physical   physically

physics

piano   pianist

piccher   picture

pich   pitch

pick [picking picked]

pick   ~axe ~pocket

pickle [pickled]

picnic   picnickers
[picnicking picnicked]

picture [pictured]

pie

piece *[part]   peace *[calm]
[piecing pieced]

pieneer   pioneer

pierce [piercing pierced]

pierse   pierce

pig   piglet

pigeon   pigeonhole

piggy   ~back ~bank

pigheaded

pigsty   pigsties

pijarmas   pyjamas

pik   pick

pikcher   picture

pile [piling piled]

pilfer [pilfering pilfered]

pilgrim   pilgrimage

pill

pillar   pillarbox

pillow   pillowcase

pilon   pylon

pilot [piloting piloted]

pimple   pimply

pin *[point]   pine *[tree, sad]

pinch [pinches pinching pinched]

pine [pining pined]

pineapple

ping-pong

pink   pinker   pinkest

pint

pioneer [pioneering]

pip *[seed]

pipe *[tube] [piping piped]

piramid   pyramid

pirate   piracy

pirote   pirate

Pisces

pistil *[flower]

pistol *[gun]

pitch   pitches [pitched]

pithon   python

pity [pities pitying pitied]

pixie

pizza

place [placing placed]

plaed   played

plague [plaguing plagued]

plain   plainly

plait *[hair]   plate *[dish]
   [plaiting plaited]

plan [planning planned]

plane *[aircraft]   plain *[basic]

planet   planetary

plank

plant [planting planted]

plasis   places

plaster [plastering plastered]

plastic

Plasticine™

plat   plait

plate *[dish]   plait *[hair]

platform

play [playing played]

play   ~ground ~group ~mate

play   ~school ~script ~time

playd   played

playful   playfully

plead [pleading pleaded]

pleasant   pleasantly

please [pleasing pleased]

pleasure   pleasurable

pleat [pleated]

pledge [pledging pledged]

pleeze   please

plenty   plentiful

plezant   pleasant

plezure   pleasure

plight *[state]   polite *[good]

plimsolls

plite   plight *[state]
            polite *[good]

plod [plodding plodded]

plot [plotting plotted]

plough [ploughing ploughed]

plow   plough

pluck [plucked]

plucky   pluckier   pluckiest

plug [plugging plugged]
plum *[fruit]   plume *[feather]
plumber   plumbing
plummer   plumber
plump   plumper   plumpest
plunder [plundered]
plunge [plunging plunged]
plus
plyte   plight
pneumonia
poach   poacher
  [poaching poached]
poak   poke
poar   paw *[foot]
              poor *[needy]
              pore *[skin, scan]
              pour *[liquid]
poch   poach
pocket   pocketful
  [pocketing pocketed]
pod
podgy   podgier   podgiest
poem
poepel   people
poet   poetic   poetical
poetry
pogy   podgy
point [pointing pointed]

pointless   pointlessly
poise [poised]
poison   poisonous
  [poisoning poisoned]
poitree   poetry
poke [poking poked]
poker
poket   pocket
pokey
polar   polar bear
pole *[stick]   poll *[vote]
pole vault
polees   police
poler   polar
police   ~man ~woman
policy   policies
poligon   polygon
polish [polishing polished]
poliss   police
polite *[good]   plight *[state]
politely   politeness
politheen   polythene
political   politician
politics
politishun   politician
poll *[vote]   pole *[stick]
pollen
pollinate [pollinated]

pollination

pollute [polluting polluted]

pollution

polo

poloot   pollute

poltry   poultry

polygon

polyte   polite

polythene

pome   poem

pompous   pompously

pond

ponder [pondered]

ponee   pony

pony   ponies

ponytail

poodle

pool *[water]   pull *[move]

pool *[collect] [pooling pooled]

poor *[needy]   paw *[foot]

           pore *[skin, scan]

           pour *[liquid]

poorer   poorest   poorly

pop [popping popped]

popcorn

Pope [the]

poplar *[tree]   popular *[liked]

poppy   poppies

popular   popularity

populated   population

por   paw *[foot]

           poor *[needy]

           pore *[skin, scan]

           pour *[liquid]

porch   porches

porcupine

pore *[skin, scan]   paw *[foot]

   [poring pored]   poor *[needy]

           pour *[liquid]

pork

pornch   paunch

porridge

porse   pause *[stop]

           paws *[feet]

porshun   portion

port   portable

porter

portion

portrait

poscher   posture

pose [posing posed]

posession   possession

posh   posher   poshest

poshun   potion

posishun   position

position [positioned]

positive   positively

possess

   [possesses possessing possessed]

possession

possessive   possessively

possibility   possibilities

possible   possibly

post [posting posted]

post   ~box ~card ~code

post   ~man ~mark ~office

postage   postage stamp

postal   postal order

poster

postige   postage

post-mortem

postpone [postponing postponed]

posture

posy   posies

posytiv   positive

pot [potting potted]

pot-belly

pot   ~hole ~holing

potato   potatoes

potenshul   potential

potential   potentially

potion

potter [pottering pottered]

pottery   potteries

pottry   pottery

pouch   pouches

poultry

pounce [pouncing pounced]

pound [pounding pounded]

pour *[liquid]   paw *[foot]

   [pouring poured] poor *[needy]

                pore *[skin, scan]

pout [pouting pouted]

poverty

powch   pouch

powder [powdered]   powdery

power [powered] powerless

powerful   powerfully

power station

pownd   pound

pownse   pounce

powt   pout

powur   power

poynt   point

poyson   poison

poze   pose

practical   practically

practice *[way]

practise *[do] [practising practised]

praer   prayer

praise [praising praised]

praktikal   practical

pram

prance [prancing pranced]

prank

pranse   prance

prawn

pray *[to God]   prey *[hunt]
  [praying prayed]

prayer

prayse   praise

preach [preaches]
  [preaching preached]

precarious   precariously

precaution

precawshun   precaution

precious

precipice

precise   precisely   precision

precocious

precorshun   precaution

predator

predict [predicting predicted]

predictable   prediction

preech   preach

preen [preening preened]

preest   priest

prefer [preferring preferred]

preferable   preferably

prefix   prefixes

pregnant   pregnancy

prehistoric

prejudice [prejudiced]

prekoshus   precocious

premature   prematurely

preoccupied

preparation   preparatory

prepare [preparing prepared]

preposition

prescribe [prescribed]

prescription

presence *[company]
  presents *[gifts]

presens   presence

present   presently
  [presenting presented]

presentation

preservation   preservative

preserve [preserving preserved]

preshure   pressure

preshus   precious

president   presidential

presise   precise

press [presses]
  [pressing pressed]

pressure   pressurised

presume [presumed]

presumably

pretect	protect
pretence	
pretend [pretending pretended]	
pretty prettier prettiest	
prevent prevention	
[preventing prevented]	
previde	provide
previous previously	
prey *[hunt]	pray *[to God]
[preying preyed]	
prezant	present
price *[cost]	prize *[award]
[pricing priced]	
priceless	
prick [pricking pricked]	
prickle [prickling prickled]	
prickly	
pride *[self-respect]	pried *[snooped]
pridict	predict

Check out **pre** as well

pridikshun	prediction
pries *[snoops]	prize *[award]
priest priestess	
prifer	prefer
prihistoric	prehistoric

prik	prick
prikul	prickle
prim primly primness	
primary	
prime [primed]	
prime minister	
prime number	
primitive	
primrose	
prince princely princess	
principal *[chief]	
principle *[rule, idea]	
prinse	prince
print [printing printed]	
priority priorities	
pripair	prepare
priscribe	prescribe
priscripshun	prescription
priservativ	preservative
prism	
prison prisoner	
prisume	presume
prisurve	preserve
pritend	pretend
prity	pretty
privacy	
private privately	
privent	prevent

privilege [privileged]

privvasee   privacy

prize *[award]   price *[cost]

probable   probably

probe [probing probed]

probible   probable

problem

proceed [proceeding proceeded]

process [processes]

  [processing processed]

procession

proclaim [proclaiming proclaimed]

prod   [prodding prodded]

produce [producing produced]

producer

product   production

produse   produce

profesee   prophecy

profeshun   profession

profession   professional

professor

profet   prophet *[seer]

              profit *[gain]

proffesor   professor

profile

profit *[gain]   prophet *[seer]

  [profiting profited]

progect   project

program *[computer]

  [programming programmed]

programme *[events]

progress [progressing progressed]

project   projector

promise [promising promised]

promiss   promise

promoshun   promotion

promote [promoted]

promotion   promotional

prompt [prompting prompted]

promptly

promt   prompt

prone

prong

pronoun

pronounce

  [pronouncing pronounced]

pronounciation   pronunciation

pronown   pronoun

pronunciation

proof *[fact]   prove *[show]

proon   prune

proov   prove

prop [propping propped]

propel [propelled] propeller

proper   properly

property   properties

prophecy *[prediction]*

prophesy *[predict]*

  [prophesies prophesied]

prophet   prophetic

proporshun   proportion

proportion

propose   proposal

  [proposing proposed]

prorn   prawn

prose

prosecute [prosecuted]

proseed   proceed

prosequte   prosecute

prosess   process

prospect

protecshun   protection

protect   protection

  [protecting protected]

protective   protectively

proteen   protein

protein

protest [protesting protested]

proud   prouder   proudest

proudly

prove *[show]*   proof *[fact]*

proverb   proverbial

provide [providing provided]

provision   provisional

provocative

provoke [provoked]

prow

prowd   proud

prowl [prowling prowled]

pruf   proof *[fact]*

          prove *[show]*

prune [pruning pruned]

pruve   prove

pry [pries prying pried]

pryde   pride

psychological

psychology   psychologist

pterodactyl

pub

puberty

public   publicity

publication

publik   public

publish   publisher

  [publishing published]

publisity   publicity

puce

pudding

puddle

pudel   puddle

puff [puffing puffed]

puffin

pule   pull

pull *[move]   pool *[water]
   [pulling pulled]

pullover

pulp [pulped]

pulpit

pulse

puma   pumas

pumel   pummel

pumkin   pumpkin

pump [pumping pumped]

pumpkin

pun

puncchual   punctual

punch [punches punching punched]

punctual   punctuality

punctuate   punctuation

puncture

punish [punishes]
   [punishing punished]

punishment

punkture   puncture

punnet

puny   punier   puniest

pupa   pupae

pupil

puppet

puppy   puppies

pur   per *[rate]

Check out
per as well

purcentage   percentage

purchase [purchased]

purcushon   percussion

purd   purred

pure *[perfect]   purr *[cat]

pure   purely

purfict   perfect

purform   perform

purfume   perfume

purhaps   perhaps

purify [purified]

purm   perm

purmanent   permanent

puroved   proved

purple

purpose   purposely

purr *[cat]   per *[rate]
   [purring purred]

purrfikt   perfect

purse

pursecutid   persecuted

pursevure   persevere

pursue [pursuing pursued]

pursuit

push [pushes pushing pushed]

put *[place] [putting put]

putt *[golf] [putting putted]

putty

puzzle [puzzling puzzled]

pyjamas

pyle   pile

Check out
pi as well

pylon

pynt   pint

pyramid

pyrit   pirate

Pysees   Pisces

python

pyur   pure

qake	quake
qarrel	quarrel
qarter	quarter
qeschun	question

quack [quacking quacked]

quadratic equation

quadrilateral

quadruple [quadrupled]

quaint quainter quaintest

quak	quack

quake [quaking quaked]

Quaker

qualification

qualify [qualifies]
  [qualifying qualified]

quality qualities

quantity quantities

quarantine

quarrel quarrelsome
  [quarrelling quarrelled]

quarry quarries

quart

quarter

quartet

quarts *[measure]*

quartz *[mineral]*

quaree	quarry
quay *[sea]*	key *[lock, main]*

que	cue *[billiards]*	
	queue *[line up]*	

queasy queasier queasiest

queen

queer queerer queerest

queerly

queery	query
queezy	queasy
queiten	quieten

quell [quelling quelled]

quench [quenching quenched]

query queries [querying queried]

quest

question [questioning questioned]

questionable

questionnaire

queue *[line]*	cue *[ball]*
[queueing queued]	

quiat	quiet

quibble [quibbling quibbled]

quick quicker quickest

quicken [quickening quickened]

quickly quickness

quicksand

quick-tempered

quick-witted

quicley	quickly

quid

quier	queer	quorrel	quarrel
quiet *[silent]	quite *[rather]	quorry	quarry
quieten [quietening quietened]		quorter	quarter
quieter quietest		quorts	quarts
quietly			*[measure]
quilt [quilted]			quartz
quirky quirkier			*[mineral]
quit *[leave, stop]		quoruntine	quarantine
[quitting quitted quit]		quota	
quite *[rather]	quiet *[silent]	quotashun	quotation
quitter		quotation	
quiver [quivering quivered]		quote [quoting quoted]	
quiz quizzes [quizzing quizzed]		qwack	quack
quodratic	quadratic	qwench	quench
		qwick	quick
		qwit	quit
		qwod	quad
		qworter	quarter
		qwote	quote

Check out
qua as well

quolify	qualify
quolity	quality
quontity	quantity

rabbit

rabeys   rabies

rabies   rabid

race *[win]   raise *[lift]
[racing raced]

racehorse

racial   racism   racist

rack *[shelf]   rake *[leaves]

racket *[din]   racquet *[bat]

radar

radiator

radio   radios

radioactive   radioactivity

radius

radyo   radio

raffle [raffling raffled]

raft [rafting rafted]

rag *[cloth]   rage *[fury]

rage *[fury] [raging raged]

ragged *[torn]   raged *[fury]

raid [raiding raided]

rail   railway

rain *[water]   reign *[rule]
[raining rained]   rein *[horse]

rain   ~coat ~drop

rain   ~fall ~forest

raindeer   reindeer

rainy   rainier   rainiest

raise *[lift]   rays *[light]
[raising raised]

raisin

raje   rage

rake

ram

ramble   rambler
[rambling rambled]

rampage [rampaged]

ramparts

ramshackled

ran

ranch   ranches

rane   rain *[water]
          reign *[rule]
          rein *[horse]

rang

range [ranging ranged]

rank   rankings

ransack [ransacking ransacked]

ransom [ransomed]

rant [ranting ranted]

rap *[knock]   wrap *[pack]
[rapping rapped]

rapper *[pop]   wrapper *[case]

rapid   rapidly

rare   rarer   rarest   rarely

rasberry   raspberry

rascal

rash rashly rashness

rashio   ratio

rashun   ration

rasisum   racism

raspberry raspberries

rat [ratted]

rate [rating rated]

rather

rattle [rattling rattled]

ratty rattier

ravenous ravenously

ravioli

raw *[uncooked] roar *[lion]

raydar   radar

rayl   rail

rayn   rain *[water]

                reign *[rule]

                rein *[horse]

rays *[light]   raise *[lift]

rayser   razor

rayshal   racial

razor

reach [reaching reached]

react [reacting reacted]

reaction

read *[book]   reed *[plant]
  [reading read]

reader

ready readier readiest

real *[actual]   reel *[spin]

realise realisation
  [realising realised]

realism realist

realistic realistically

reality

really *[truly]   rely *[trust]

reap   reaper [reaping reaped]

reappear reappearance
  [reappearing reappeared]

rear *[horse]   rare *[scarce]
  [rearing reared]

rearrange [rearranged]

reason [reasoned]

reasonable reasonably

reassure reassurance
  [reassuring reassured]

rebal   rebel

rebel rebellion
  [rebelling rebelled]

rebellious rebelliously

rebild   rebuild

rebuild [rebuilding rebuilt]

rebuke [rebuked]

recall [recalling recalled]

recede [receding receded]

174

receipt

receive   receiver
  [receiving received]

recent *[latest]   resent *[grudge]

recently

reception   receptionist

receptive

rech   reach *[get]
                   retch *[vomit]
                   wretch *[person]

recipe   recipes

recite   recital [reciting recited]

reckless   recklessly

recklessness

reckon [reckoning reckoned]

reclaim [reclaiming reclaimed]

recline [reclining reclined]

recognise   recognisable
  [recognising recognised]

recognition

recoil [recoiling recoiled]

recollect   recollection
  [recollecting recollected]

recommend   recommendation
  [recommending recommended]

reconcile [reconciled]

reconciliation

reconnect [reconnected]

reconsider
  [reconsidering reconsidered]

reconsile   reconcile

reconstruct [reconstructed]

record [recording recorded]

recover   recoverable
  [recovering recovered]

recovery   recoveries

recreation   recreational

recruit   recruitment
  [recruiting recruited]

rectangle   rectangular

recur [recurring recurred]

recurrence   recurrent

recycle [recycled]

red *[colour]   read *[book]

redden [reddening]

reddy   ready

redial [redialling redialled]

redo [redoing redone]

redouble [redoubled]

reduce   reduction
  [reducing reduced]

redundancy   redundant

reduse   reduce

reech   reach

reed *[plant]   read *[book]

reek *[smell]   wreak *[havoc]

reel *[spin]   real *[true]

reeson   reason

refer [referring referred]

referee [refereeing refereed]

reference [referenced]

refill   refillable [refilling refilled]

refine [refined]   refinement

reflect   reflective

   [reflecting reflected]

reflection

reflex   reflexes

refrain [refrained]

refresh   refreshment

   [refreshing refreshed]

refrigerate [refrigerated]

refrigeration   refrigerator

refuel [refuelling refuelled]

refuge *[shelter]

refugee *[flee]   refugees

refund [refunding refunded]

refuree   referee

refuse   refusal [refusing refused]

regain [regaining regained]

regard   regardless

   [regarding regarded]

regatta   regattas

regay   reggae

regect   reject

reggae

regiment   regimental

region   regional

register   registration

   [registering registered]

regler   regular

regret [regretting regretted]

regretful   regretfully

regrettable   regrettably

regular   regularly   regularity

rehearse   rehearsal

   [rehearsing rehearsed]

reheat [reheating reheated]

reign *[rule]   rain *[water]

            rein *[horse]

   [reigning reigned]

rein *[horse]   rain *[water]

            reign *[rule]

reindeer

reinforce   reinforcement

   [reinforcing reinforced]

reject [rejecting rejected]

rejection

rejiment   regiment

rejister   register

rejoice [rejoicing rejoiced]

rejuce   reduce

rejun   region

rekollekt   recollect

rekommend   recommend

rekord   record

rekwest   request

relate [relating related]

relation   relationship

relative   relatively

relavent   relevant

relax   relaxation
  [relaxes relaxing relaxed]

relay [relaying relayed]

release [releasing released]

relegate   relegation
  [relegating relegated]

relent [relenting relented]

relentless   relentlessly

relevance   relevant

reliable   reliably

relief

relieve [relieved]

religion

religious   religiously

relijion   religion

relly   really

reluctance

reluctant   reluctantly

rely *[trust]   really *[truly]
  [relies relying relied]

remain   remainder
  [remaining remained]

remark   remarkable
  [remarking remarked]

rember   remember

remember
  [remembering remembered]

remind   reminder
  [reminding reminded]

remote   remoter

remotely   remoteness

remove   removal
  [removing removed]

rendezvous

renew [renewing renewed]

renewable

repair [repairing repaired]

repay   repayment
  [repaying repaid]

repayd   repaid

repeat [repeating repeated]

repeatedly

repel [repelled]   repellent

repent [repenting repented]

repere   repair

repete   repeat

repetition   repetitious

repetitive   repetitively

replace   replaceable
[replacing replaced]

replacement

replay [replaying replayed]

reply   replies [replying replied]

report   reportedly   reporter
[reporting reported]

represent   representation
[representing represented]

representative

reprimand [reprimanded]

reproduce
[reproducing reproduced]

reproduction   reproductive

reptile   reptilian

repulsive   repulsively

reputation

request [requesting requested]

require   requirement
[requiring required]

rere   rare *[scarce]
                    rear *[back,
                        horse]

rerite   rewrite

rerote   rewrote

resalootion   resolution

rescue   rescuer
[rescuing rescued]

research [researches]
[researching researched]

resseet   receipt

reseeve   receive

resemble [resembling resembled]

resemblance

resent *[grudge]   recent *[latest]

resentful   resentment

resepshun   reception

reservation

reserve [reserved]

reservoir

residence   resident

residenchal   residential

residential

resign   resignation
[resigning resigned]

resipy   recipe

resist [resisting resisted]

resistance   resistant

resite   recite

reskue   rescue

resle   wrestle

resolution

resolve [resolving resolved]

resons   reasons

resort [resorting resorted]

resource   resourceful

respect   respectable
  [respecting respected]
respectful   respectfully
respond [responded]
response   responsibility
responsibilities
responsible   responsibly
resstront   restaurant
rest [resting rested]
restaurant
restful   restfully
restless   restlessly
restore   restoration
  [restoring restored]
restrain   restraint
  [restraining restrained]
restrict   restriction
  [restricting restricted]
result [resulting resulted]
resurvwa   reservoir
resuscitate [resuscitated]
resuscitation
resycle   recycle
retain [retaining retained]
retaliate [retaliated]
retch *[vomit] [retching]
  wretch *[person]
rethink [rethinking rethought]

retire   retirement
  [retiring retired]
retort [retorting retorted]
retrace [retracing retraced]
retreat [retreating retreated]
retrieve   retrievable
  [retrieving retrieved]
retriever
retrospect   retrospective
return [returning returned]
reunion
reunite [reuniting reunited]
reveal [revealing revealed]
revenge   revengeful
reverse   reversible
  [reversing reversed]
review [reviewed]
revise [revising revised]
revision
revive [reviving revived]
revolt [revolting revolted]
revolution   revolutionary
revolutionise [revolutionised]
revolve [revolving revolved]
revolver
reward [rewarding rewarded]
rewind [rewinding rewound]
rezzavwa   reservoir

rfter	after
rfternon	afternoon
rheumatism	
rhino rhinoceros	
rhomboid rhombus	
rhubarb	
rhyme [rhyming rhymed]	
rhythm rhythmical	
riacshun	reaction
riact	react
riality	reality
rib	
ribbon	
ribellius	rebellious
rice *[food]	rise *[up]
riceipt	receipt
rich richly richness	
Richter Scale [the]	
rickety	
riclaim	reclaim
ricoil	recoil
rid riddance	
riddle	
ride rider [riding rode ridden]	
ridge ridged	
ridiculous ridiculously	
rifle [rifling rifled]	
riflect	reflect

right *[correct]	write *[pen]
right rightly rightful	
right-handed	
rigid rigidly	
rim *[edge]	rhyme *[poetry]
rimless rimmed	
rimain	remain

Check out re as well

rimark	remark
rimember	remember
rimote	remote
rimoval	removal
rind	
ring *[circle]	wring *[wet]
ring *[bell] [ringing rang rung]	
rink	
rinkle	wrinkle
rino	rhino
rinse [rinsing rinsed]	
riot [rioting rioted]	
riotous riotously	
rip *[tear]	ripe *[ready]
[ripping ripped]	
ripair	repair
ripe ripeness	
ripeat	repeat

ripen [ripening ripened]

riply   **reply**

riport   **report**

ripple [rippling rippled]

ripulsiv   **repulsive**

riquest   **request**

riquire   **require**

rise *[up]*   **rice** *[food]*

   [rises rising risen]

riserve   **reserve**

risine   **resign**

risist   **resist**

risk [risking risked]

risky   riskier   riskiest

risolve   **resolve**

risort   **resort**

risotto

risource   **resource**

rispect   **respect**

rispectabul   **respectable**

risponsibul   **responsible**

ritch   **rich**

rithum   **rhythm**

ritual

riturn   **return**

rival   rivalry

rivenge   **revenge**

river   riverside

rivet [riveting riveted]

ro   **roe** *[deer]*

             row *[boat]*

road *[street]*   **rode** *[bike]*

             rowed *[boat]*

roam *[wander]*   **Rome** *[city]*

   [roaming roamed]

roar *[lion]*   **raw** *[uncooked]*

   [roaring roared]

roast [roasting roasted]

rob [robbed]   **robbery**

robe [robed]

robin

robot   robotic

rock [rocking rocked]

rocket

rocky   rockier   rockiest

rod *[fishing]*   **rode** *[bike]*

             road *[street]*

             rowed *[boat]*

rodent

roial   **royal**

rok   **rock**

roket   **rocket**

role *[actor]*

roll *[move]* [rolling rolled]   **roller**

Roman   Roman Catholic

romance

romanse   romance

romantic   romantically

rombus   rhombus

Romen   Roman

rondayvoo   rendezvous

rong   wrong

roobarb   rhubarb

roof   roofless

rook   rookery

room   roomful   roomy

roomer   rumour

roost [roosting roosted]

rooster

root *[plant]   route *[way]
  [rooting rooted]

rooteen   routine

rope [roped]

rore   roar *[lion]
                raw *[fresh]

rose *[flower]   rows *[boat]

rosette

rost   roast

rosy

rot [rotting rotted]

rota *[list]   rotor *[blade]

rotashun   rotation

rotate [rotating rotated]

rotation

rote *[repeat]   wrote *[pen]

rotor *[blade]   rota *[list]

rotten

rough   rougher   roughly

round   rounder   roundly

roundabout

rounders

route *[way]   root *[plant]

routine

row *[boat] [rowing rowed]

row *[noise] [rowed]   rowdy

rownd   round

rows *[boat]   rose *[flower]

royal   royally   royalty

rub [rubbing rubbed]

rubarb   rhubarb

rubber   rubbery

rubbish [rubbished]   rubbishy

rubble

ruby   rubies

rucksack

rudder

rude   ruder   rudest

rude   rudely   rudeness

ruel   rule

Rugby League   Rugby Union

rugged

ruin [ruining ruined]

rule   ruler [ruling ruled]

rumatic   rheumatic

rumatisum   rheumatism

rumble [rumbling rumbled]

rumour   [rumoured]

rumple [rumpled]

run [running ran]   runner

rung *[ring]   wrung *[wet]

runny   runnier   runniest

runway

rush [rushing rushed]

Rushun   Russian

russel   rustle

rust   rusted   rusty

rustle   rustler
  [rustling rustled]

rut [rutted]

rute   root *[plant]
              route *[way]

ruthless   ruthlessly

ruthlessness

ryce   rice

ryme   rhyme

ryval   rival

sabbath

sachel   satchel

sack [sacking sacked]

sacrifice   sacrificial
   [sacrificing sacrificed]

sad   sadder   sadly   sadness

sadden [saddening saddened]

saddle [saddling saddled]

safari   safaris

safe   safer   safely

safety

saffire   sapphire

saftey   safety

sag [sagging sagged]   saggy

said

saif   safe

sail *[boat]   sale *[goods]
   [sailing sailed]

sailor

saim   same

saint   saintly

saiv   save

sak   sack *[bag,
             destroy]
         sake *[sake of]

sake

sakrifise   sacrifice

salad

salary   salaries

sale *[goods]   sail *[boat]

salery   salary

sales   ~man ~person ~woman

saliva

salmon

salon

salt   salty   saltier

salute [saluting saluted]

salvage   [salvaged]

salvige   salvage

Samaritan

same   sameness

samon   salmon

sample [sampling sampled]

sand [sanding sanded]

sandbank   sandpit

sandwich   sandwiches

sandy   sandier   sandiest

sane   sanely   saner

sanity

sank

Santa Claus

sanwich   sandwich

sapphire

sarcastic   sarcastically

sardine

sari

sarkastik	sarcastic
sarm	psalm
sat	
Satan	Satanic
satchel	
satellite	
Saterday	Saturday
satisfactory	
satisfy	satisfaction
[satisfying satisfied]	
Saturday	
sauce *[dip]	source *[start]
saucepan	
saucer	
sauna	
saunter [sauntering sauntered]	
sausage	
sause	sauce *[liquid]
	source *[origin]
savage savagely	
[savaging savaged]	
save [saving saved] saver	
savige	savage
saviour	
saw *[see]	soar *[fly]
	sore *[hurt]
saw *[cut] [sawn] sawdust	
saxophone saxophonist	

say [saying said]	
saym	same
saynt	saint
sayvyer	saviour
scab scabby scabbier	
scaffold scaffolding	
scair	scare
scald [scalding scalded]	
scale [scaling scaled]	
scalp [scalped]	
scalpel	
scaly scalier scaliest	
scam	
scamper [scampered]	
scampi	
scan [scanning scanned]	
scandal scandalous	
scanner	
scar *[mark]	scare *[shock]
scarce scarcely scarcity	
scare *[shock]	scar *[mark]
scarecrow	
scarf scarves	
scarlet	
scarse	scarce
scary scarier scariest	
scate	skate
scatter [scattering scattered]	

scatty   scattier   scattiest

scavenge   scavenger
  [scavenging scavenged]

scaw   score

scene *[stage]   seen *[eyes]

scenery

scent *[smell]   sent *[gone]
                    cent *[money]

scerd   scared

scery   scary

schedule [scheduled]

scholar   scholarship

school   ~boy ~child ~girl

science   scientist

scientific   scientifically

scill   skill

scin   skin

scip   skip

scissors

scoff [scoffing scoffed]

scolar   scholar

scold *[tell off]   scald *[burn]

scone

scool   school

scoop [scooped]

scoot   scooter

scorch [scorching scorched]

score [scored]   scoreboard

scorpion

Scot   Scotch   Scottish

scout [scouted]

scowl [scowling scowled]

scrabble [scrabbled]

scrach   scratch

scramble [scrambled]

scrap *[junk] [scrapped]

scrape *[remove]

scratch [scratches]
  [scratching scratched]

scratchy   scratchier

scrawl [scrawled]

scrawny   scrawnier

screach   screech

scream

screech   screeches
  [screeching screeched]

screen   screenwriter

screme   scream

screw [screwed] screwdriver

screwpel   scruple

scribble   scribbler
  [scribbling scribbled]

scribe

scripcher   scripture

script   scriptwriter

scripture

scroll [scrolled]

scroo   screw

scrooge

scrornee   scrawny

scrounge   scrounger

scrownge   scrounge

scrub [scrubbing scrubbed]

scruff   scruffy   scruffier

scrum

scrunch [scrunches]
   [scrunching scrunched]

scuba

scuff [scuffing scuffed]

scuffle [scuffling scuffled]

sculpcher   sculpture

sculpt [sculpted]

sculptor *[artist]

sculpture *[carving]

scum   scummy

scurry [scurrying scurried]

scuttle [scuttled]

scwelchey   squelchy

sea *[waves]   see *[eyes]

sea-anenome

sea   ~front ~gull ~horse

sea   ~shore ~sick ~side

sead   said *[say]
          seed *[plant]

seak   seek *[look for]
          Sikh *[religion]

seal [sealing sealed]

Check out ce as well

sealing   ceiling *[roof]
   *[fastening]

seam *[cloth]   seem *[appear]

sean   scene *[stage]
         seen *[eyes]

search [searches searched]

searching   searchlight

seasaw   seesaw

sease   cease *[stop]
         seize *[grab]

season   seasonal

seat [seating seated]

secendry   secondary

second   secondly

secondary

secrecy

secretary   secretaries

secure [secured]   securely

security

sed   said

see *[eyes]   sea *[waves]
   [seeing saw seen]

seekrit   secret
seed [seeded]   seedling
seel   seal
seeling   ceiling
seem *[appear]   seam *[cloth]
  [seeming seemed]
seen *[see]   scene *[stage]
seereez   series
seeriul   cereal
seesaw [seesawed]
seeson   season
seet   seat
seid   said
seize *[grab]   cease *[stop]
sekure   secure
sekwence   sequence
sekwin   sequin
seldom
selebrate   celebrate
select [selecting selected]
selection   selective
selery   celery
self   selves
selfish   selfishly
selfless   selflessly
sell *[shop]   cell *[prison]
seller *[sales   cellar *[room]
      person]

Sellotape™
Selsius   Celsius
selves
seme   seam *[cloth]
                 seem *[appear]
sement   cement
semetery   cemetery
semi   ~circle ~circular
semi   ~colon ~conscious
semi-final
send [sending sent]   sender
sene   scene *[stage]
                 seen *[eyes]
sensashunal   sensational
sensation   sensational
sense   senseless
sensible   sensibly
sensitive   sensitively
sensitivity   sensitivities
sent *[gone]   scent *[smell]
senta   centre
sentence
sentens   sentence
senter   centre

Check out
ce as well

sentigrade   centigrade

188

sentimental   sentimentality
sentimetre   centimetre
sentipede   centipede
sentral   central
sentry   sentries
sentury   century
separate   seperately
separation
sepret   separate
September
sequence   sequential
sequin [sequinned]
ser   sir
seramic   ceramic
serch   search
serchin   searching
sereal   cereal *[grain]
                serial
                    *[sequence]
seremonee   ceremony
serf *[slave]   surf *[sea]
serface   surface
sergeant
sergeon   surgeon
serial *[sequence] cereal *[grain]
serialisation [serialising]
series
serious   seriously

sermon
sername   surname
serpent
serprise   surprise
sertain   certain
sertificate   certificate
servant
serve [serving served]
service [serviced]
sesshun   session
session
set *[put]   seat *[sitting]
                sett *[badger]
setentes   sentences
settee
setting
settle [settling settled]
seveir   severe
seven   seventeen   seventh
sevon   seven
seventy   seventieth
several
severe   severely   severity
sevnteen   seventeen
sevrel   several
sew *[clothes]   sow *[seed]
  [sewing sewn]   so *[thus]
sewer   sewerage

sewn *[clothes]   sown *[seed]

sex

sey   say

sfere   sphere

shabby shabbier

shack

shackle [shackled]

shade shaded shady

shadow shadowy

shaft

shaggy shaggier

shaid   shade

shaip   shape

shair   share

shake [shaking shaken]

shaky shakier

shall

shallow shallower

shamble shambles

shame *[guilt]   sham *[fake]

shameful shamefully

shameless shamelessly

shampain   champagne

shampoo [shampooed]

shan't [shall not]

shape shapeless shapely

shark shark-infested

sharp sharply sharpness

sharpen sharpener
  [sharpening sharpened]

shatter [shattered]

shave [shaving shaved]

shaw   shore *[sea]

                  sure *[certain]

shawl

shawt   short

she she's [she is, has]

shear *[clip]   sheer *[steep]

shed *[hut, hair]

she'd *[she had, would]

shedule   schedule

sheep sheepish sheepishly

sheer *[steep]   shear *[clip]

sheet sheeting

sheild   shield

shelf shelves

shell [sea]   she'll *[she will]

shelter [sheltering sheltered]

shepherd

sheriff

shert   shirt

she's [she is, she has]

shi   she *[female]

                  shy *[timid]

shield [shielding shielded]

shier   sheer

shiffon   chiffon

shift [shifting shifted]   **shifty**

shimmer   shimmery
  [shimmering shimmered]

shin *[leg]

shine *[sun] [shining shone]

shingle   shingly

shiny   shinier   shiniest

ship [shipping shipped]

shipwreck [shipwrecked]

shirk [shirking shirked]

shirt

shiver   shivery
  [shivering shivered]

sho   show

shoal

shoar   shore *[sea]
                sure *[certain]

shock [shocking shocked]

shoddy   shoddier

shoe *[foot]   shoo *[away]
  [shoes shoing shoed]

shoe ~horn ~lace

shofer   chauffeur

shok   shock

sholder   shoulder

shone *[lit up,   shown
       polished]   *[did show]

shoo *[away]   shoe *[foot]
  [shooes shooing shooed]

shood   should

shook

shool   school

shoot *[target]   chute *[slide]
  [shooting shot]

shoow   shoe

shop [shopping shopped]

shoplifter [shoplifting]

shore *[sea]   sure *[certain]

shorn

short   shortly   shortness

shortage

shorten [shortened]

shot

should

shouldent   shouldn't

shoulder

shouldn't [should not]

shout [shouting shouted]

shove [shoving shoved]

shovel [shovelling shovelled]

show [showing showed]

shower   showery

showt   shout

showy   showier   showiest

shrank

shred   shredder
[shredding shredded]

shreik   shriek

shrew   shrewish

shrewd   shrewdly

shrewdness

shriek [shrieking shrieked]

shrill   shrilly

shrimp [shrimping]

shrink [shrinking shrunk]

shrivel [shrivelled]

Shrove Tuesday

shrub   shrubbery

shrued   shrewd

shrug [shrugging shrugged]

shrunk   shrunken

shud   should

shudder [shuddering shuddered]

shudent   shouldn't
                         [should not]

shuffle   shuffly
[shuffling shuffled]

shun [shunned]

shunt [shunting shunted]

shut *[close]   chute *[slide]
[shutting shut]

shuttle

shuv   shove

shuvel   shovel

shy *[timid]   shyly   shyness

shy *[horse] [shies shying shied]

si   sigh

siad   said

Siamese

sichuayshun   situation

sick *[ill]   Sikh *[religion]

sicken [sickening sickened]

side [siding sided]

side ~burns ~ways

sider   cider

sidle [sidling sidled]

sied   sighed

siege

siense   science

sieve [sieved]

sift [sifting sifted]

sigaret   cigarette

sigh [sighing sighed]

sight *[see]   site *[place]

sightseeing   sightseer

sign   signpost

signachure   signature

signal [signalled]

signature

signet *[ring]   cygnet *[swan]

significant   significantly

sik	sick
Sikh *[religion]	seek *[look]
siksth	sixth
silee	silly
silence silencer	
[silencing silenced]	
silent silently	
silhouette	
silk silken silky	
sillabul	syllable
sillooet	silhouette
silly sillier silliest	
silver silvery	
simbol	cymbal *[music]
	symbol *[sign]
simese	Siamese
similar similarity	
simmer [simmering]	
simmetrical	symmetrical
simpathetic	sympathetic
simple simpler simplest	
simplicity simply	
simplify [simplifies]	
[simplifying simplified]	
simpul	simple
since *[from]	sins *[bad]
sincere sincerely sincerity	
sindrome	syndrome

sinema	cinema
sinful sinfully	
sing *[music]	singer
[singing sang]	
singe *[burn] [singeing singed]	
single singly	
sinister	
sink [sinking sank sunk]	
sinmer	cinema
sinner	
sinonim	synonym
sinse	since
sip [sipping sipped]	
sir	

Check out
cir as well

sircul	circle
sircus	circus
siren	
siringe	syringe
sirrup	syrup
sise	size
sissors	scissors
sissy sissies	
sister sisterly	
sistes	sisters
sit [sitting sat]	

site *[place]   sight *[seeing]

siteseeing   sightseeing

sitizen   citizen

sitrus   citrus

situate [situated]

situation

sity   city

sityooashun   situation

sive   sieve

sivil   civil

sivilisashun   civilisation

six   sixth

sixteen   sixteenth

sixty   sixtieth

size   sizeable

sizzle [sizzling sizzled]

skab   scab

skaffold   scaffold

skale   scale

skalp   scalp

skaly   scaly

skate [skating skated]

skateboard   skateboarder

skeleton   skeletal

skert   skirt

sketch   sketches
  [sketching sketched]

sketchy   sketchier

skewer [skewered]

ski *[sport]   sky *[air]
  [skis skiing skied]

skid *[slip]   skied *[sport]
  [skidding skidded]

skilful   skilfully

skill [skilled]

skim [skimming skimmed]

skin [skinned]

skinny   skinnier   skinniest

skint

skip [skipping skipped]

skirt [skirting skirted]

skittle

skold   scald *[burn]
                    scold *[tell off]

skon   scone

skool   school

skript   script

skufful   scuffle

skull

skuttling   scuttling

skwall   squall

skware   square

skwobble   squabble

skwod   squad

skwodron   squadron

skwonder   squander

skwosh	squash
skwot	squat
sky *[space]	ski *[sport]
sky ~scraper ~wards	
slab	
slack slacker slackest	
slaiv	slave
slam [slamming slammed]	
slander slanderous	
slang slanging match	
slant [slanting slanted]	
slap [slapping slapped]	
slash [slashing slashed]	
slate	
slaughter [slaughtered]	
slave slavery	
slay [slaying slew slain]	
sleap	sleep
sleat	sleet
sleave	sleeve
sledge sledging	
sleek sleekly sleekness	
sleep [sleeping slept]	
sleepless sleeplessness	
sleepy sleepier sleepiest	
sleet sleeting	
sleeve sleeveless	
slege	sledge

sleigh *[snow]	slay *[kill]
slender slenderness	
slep	sleep
slepin	sleeping
slept	
sley	slay *[kill]
	sleigh *[snow]
slice [slicing sliced]	
slick slickly slickness	
slide [sliding slid]	
slied	slide
slight slightly	
slik	slick
slim *[thin]	
slime *[gooey] slimy	
sling [slinging slung]	
slip [slipping slipped]	
slipper	
slippery slippy slippier	
slise	slice
slit slitty	
slither [slithered] slithery	
slobber slobbery	
[slobbering slobbered]	
slog [slogging slogged]	
slooth	sleuth
slope [sloping sloped]	
slorter	slaughter

slot [slotting slotted]

slouch [slouching slouched]

slow   slower   slowly

sludge   sludgy

slug   sluggish   sluggishly

slum   slummy

slumber [slumbering slumbered]

slump [slumped]

slung

slurp [slurping slurped]

slush   slushy

sly   slyly   slyness

slymee   slimy

smack [smacking smacked]

small   smaller   smallest

smart   smarter   smartest

smartly   smartness

smash [smashing smashed]

smear [smearing smeared]

smell [smelling smelt]

smelly   smellier   smelliest

smile [smiling smiled]

smiley   smilier   smiliest

smithereens

smog   smoggy

smoke [smoking smoked]

smoky   smokier   smokiest

smooth [smoothing smoothed]

smoothie

smoothly   smoothness

smother [smothering smothered]

smoulder

 [smouldering smouldered]

smudge   smudged   smudgy

smug   smugly   smugness

smuggle   smuggler

 [smuggling smuggled]

smyle   smile

snack [snacking snacked]

snaik   snake

snail

snair   snare

snak   snack

snake [snaking]   snakey

snale   snail

snap [snapping snapped]

snare [snaring snared]

snarl [snarling snarled]

snatch [snatches]

 [snatching snatched]

sneaky   sneakier   sneakiest

sneer [sneering sneered]

sneeze [sneezing sneezed]

snifel   sniffle

sniff [sniffing sniffed]

sniffle [sniffling sniffled]

snigger [sniggering sniggered]

snip [snipped]

sniper

snivel [snivelling snivelled]

sno   snow

snob   snobbery

snooker [snookered]

snoop [snooping snooped]

snooty

snooze [snoozing snoozed]

snorcul   snorkel

snore [snoring snored]

snorkel [snorkelling]

snort [snorting snorted]

snout

snow [snowing snowed]

snow   ~ball ~boarding ~bound

snow   ~drift ~drop ~fall

snow   ~flake ~man ~plough

snow   ~shoes ~storm

snowt   snout

snowy   snowier   snowiest

snub [snubbing snubbed]

snuff [snuffed]

snuffle [snuffling snuffled]

snuffly

snug   snuggle   snuggly
   [snuggling snuggled]

snuze   snooze

so *[thus]   sew *[clothes]

               sow *[seeds]

soak [soaking soaked]

soal   sole *[one]

          soul *[spirit]

soap   soapy   soapier

soar *[fly]   saw *[see, cut]

          sore *[hurt]

sob [sobbing sobbed]

soccer

social   sociable   socially

sock

socker   soccer

socket

soda

sodden

sofa

soffen   soften

soft   softly   softness

soften [softened]

software

soggy   soggier   soggiest

soil [soiling soiled]

sok   sock *[foot]

          soak *[water]

solar

sold

solder *[metal] [soldering]

soldier *[army] [soldiering]

sole *[one]   soul *[spirit]

solejur   soldier

solem   solemn

solemn   solemnly

soler   solar

solger   soldier

solicitor

solid   solidly

solitary

solo   soloist

solt   salt

solution

solve [solving solved]

som   some

some *[amount]   sum *[add]

some   ~body ~how ~one ~thing

some   ~times ~what ~where

somersault [somersaulted]

son *[boy]   sun *[shine]

song

sonic

soon   sooner   soonest

soop   soup

soor   saw

soot *[coal]   suit *[clothes]

soothe [soothing soothed]

sooty   sootier   sootiest

sopey   soapy

sopping

soppy   soppier   soppiest

sor   sore

sorce   sauce *[liquid]

          source *[origin]

sorcer   saucer

sorcerer   sorceress   sorcery

sord   sword

sordust   sawdust

sore *[hurt]   saw *[see, cut]

          soar *[fly]

sorely

sorn   sawn

sorna   sauna

soro   sorrow

sorrow   sorrowful

sorrowfully

sorry   sorrier   sorriest

sorserer   sorcerer

sort *[kind]   sought *[seek]

sory   sorry

soshabul   sociable

soshall   social

sosiety   society

sossige   sausage

sought *[seek]   sort *[kind]

soul *[spirit]   sole *[one]

sound   soundly
  [sounding sounded]

soundless   soundlessly

soup

sour   sourly   sourness

source *[start]   sauce *[dip]

south   southern   southerner

souvenir

sovereign

sovren   sovereign

sow *[seed]   sew *[clothes]

sow *[pig]   so *[thus]

sown *[seed]   sewn *[clothes]

sownd   sound

sowr   sour

sowth   south

space [spacing spaced]

space ~man ~ship ~suit

spade

spagety   spaghetti

spaghetti

spair   spare

spam

span [spanning spanned]

spaner   spanner

spangle [spangled]

spaniel

spank [spanking spanked]

spanner

spanyel   spaniel

spare [sparing spared]

spark [sparking sparked]

sparkeling   sparkling

sparkle   sparkly
  [sparkling sparkled]

sparrow   sparrowhawk

spase   space

spatter [spattering spattered]

speach   speech

speak [speaking spoke]

spear   spearmint

special   specially

species

speckle   speckled

spectacles   spectacled

spectacular   spectacularly

spectator

speech   speechless

speed [speeding sped]

speedometer

speedy   speedier   speediest

speek   speak

speer   spear

speesheez   species

spektakular   spectacular

199

spell [spelling spelt]

spellbinding   spellbound

spend [spending spent]

spensiv   expensive

speshul   special

sphere   spherical

spice   spiced   spicy

spider   spidery

spied

spike [spiking spiked]

spikey   spikier   spikiest

spill [spilling spilt]

spin *[turn]   spine *[back]
  [spinning spun]

spinach

spine *[back]   spin *[turn]

spineless   spinelessly

spinich   spinach

spining   spinning

spiral

spire

spise   spice

spit *[saliva] [spitting spat]

spite *[nasty]

spiteful   spitefully

splash [splashing splashed]

splashy   splashier

splatter [splattered]

splender   splendour

splendid   splendidly

splendour

splinter [splintered]

split [splitting]

splodge   splodgy

splutter [spluttering spluttered]

spoak   spoke

spoil [spoiling spoilt]

spoiler

spoke   spoken   spokesman

sponge [sponging sponged]

spongy   spongier   spongiest

spook [spooked]

spooky   spookier   spookiest

spoon [spooning spooned]

spoonful

sport [sporting sported]

sporty   sportier   sportiest

sportsman   sportswoman

spot [spotting spotted]

spotless   spotlessly

spotlight [spotlit]

spotty   spottier   spottiest

spout [spouting spouted]

sprain

sprang

sprawl [sprawled]

spray [spraying sprayed]

spread [spreading spread]

spred   spread

spring [springing sprang sprung]

spring   springtime

springy   springier

sprinkle   sprinkler

   [sprinkling sprinkled]

sprint [sprinting sprinted]

sprinter

spritely

sprout [sprouting sprouted]

sprung

spruys   surprise

spuk   spook

spur [spurred]

spurt [spurting spurted]

sputter [sputtering sputtered]

spy [spies spying spied]

spyke   spike

spyne   spine

spyral   spiral

spyre   spire

squabble [squabbling squabbled]

squad   squadron

squall   squally   squallier

squander

   [squandering squandered]

square   squarely

squash [squashing squashed]

squashy   squashier

squat [squatting squatted]

squawk [squawking squawked]

squeak [squeaking squeaked]

squeaky

squeakier   squeakiest

squeal [squealing squealed]

squeek   squeak

squeeze [squeezing squeezed]

squelch   squelchy

   [squelching squelched]

squerm   squirm

squert   squirt

squid

squiggle   squiggly

squint [squinting squinted]

squirel   squirrel

squirm [squirming squirmed]

squirrel

squirt [squirting squirted]

squish [squished]   squishy

squork   squawk

stab [stabbing stabbed]

stabel   stable

stabilisers

stable

stachue   statue

stack [stacking stacked]

stadium

staek   stake *[post]

    steak *[beef]

staer   stair *[step]

    stare *[gaze]

staff [staffing staffed]

stag *[deer]

stage *[time, theatre]

stagger [staggering staggered]

stagnant

stail   stale

stain [staining stained]

stair *[step]   stare *[gaze]

stait   state

stak   stack

stake *[post]   steak *[beef]

stalactite *[down]

stalagmite *[up]

stale   stalemate

stalegmite   stalagmite *[up]

stalektite   stalactite
                         *[down]

stalk *[follow]   stork *[bird]
   [stalking stalked]

stalker

stall [stalling stalled]

stallion

stalyen   stallion

stamp [stamping stamped]

stampede [stampeding]

stand [standing stood]

stand-offish

stane   stain

stank

stapel   staple

staple [stapled]   stapler

star *[sky]   stare *[gaze]

starboard

stare *[gaze]   stair *[step]

staree   starry

starlight   starlit

starling

starred   starry   starrier

start [starting started]

startle [startling startled]

starve   starvation
   [starving starved]

stash [stashed]

stashun   station

state [stating stated]

statement   statesman

station   stationmaster

stationary *[still]

stationery *[paper]

statue

stay [staying stayed]

stayje   stage

steady   steadier   steadiest

steak *[beef]   stake *[post]

steal *[take]   steel *[iron]

   [stealing stole stolen]

stealth   stealthy

steam [steaming steamed]

steamy   steamier   steamiest

stedy   steady

steel *[iron]   steal *[take]

steep   steeply   steepness

steeple   ~chase   ~jack

steer [steering steered]

stencil   stencilling

stensil   stencil

step [stepping stepped]

ster   stir

stern   sternly   sternness

stew [stewing stewed]

steward   stewardess

stewdent   student

stich   stitch

stick [sticking stuck]

sticker

sticky   stickier   stickiest

stier   steer

stiff   stiffer   stiffest

stiffen [stiffened]

stiffly   stiffness

stik   stick

stiky   sticky

stile *[step]   style *[type]

still   stiller   stillness

stilts

sting [stinging stung]

stingy   stingier   stingiest

stink [stinking stank stunk]

stir [stirring stirred]

stirrup

stitch   stitches

   [stitching stitched]

stoal   stole

stoan   stone

stoat

stocking

stodge   stodgy   stodgier

stole   stolen

stomach   stomach-ache

stomp [stomping stomped]

stone   Stone Age

stony   stonier   stoniest

stood

stool

stoop [stooping stooped]

stop [stopping stopped]

stopper

stopt — stopped

store [storing stored]

storey *[floor]   story *[tale]

stork *[bird]   stalk *[follow]

storm   stormy   stormier

story *[tale]   storey *[floor]

storyteller   storytelling

stout   stouter   stoutest

stoutly   stoutness

stove

stowt — stout

straey — stray

straggle   straggly
  [straggling straggled]

straight   straighter

straightforward

straighten   straightened

strain [straining strained]

strand   stranded

strane — strain

strange   strangely

stranger

strangle   strangler
  [strangling strangled]

straw

strawberry   strawberries

stray [straying strayed]

strayt — straight

streak   streaky   streakier
  [streaking streaked]

stream   streamer
  [streaming streamed]

strech — stretch

streem — stream

street   streetwise

strength

strengthen [strengthened]

strenth — strength

stress   stressed   stressful

stressfully

stretch   stretches
  [stretching stretched]

stretcher

strict   stricter   strictest

strictly   strictness

stride [striding strode]

strike [striking struck]

strikt — strict

string   stringing   stringy

stripe   striped   stripey

stroad — strode

strobrey — strawberry

strode

stroke [stroking stroked]

stroll [strolling strolled]

strong   stronger   strongly

strop   stroppy   stroppier

stror   straw

strorbury   strawberry

struck

struggle [struggling struggled]

strung

stryke   strike

stub [stubbed]

stubble   stubbly

stubborn   stubbornly

stubbornness

stubel   stubble

stuck   stuck-up

student

studio

study   studies [studying studied]

studyo   studio

stue   stew

stuff [stuffing stuffed]

stuffy   stuffier   stuffiest

stule   stool

stumack   stomach

stumble   stumbled

stumok   stomach

stun [stunning stunned]

stung

stunk

stupendous

stunt   stuntman

stupid   stupider   stupidest

stupidly   stupidity

stur   stir

sturn   stern

stutter   stutterer
  [stuttering stuttered]

sty   sties

style *[type]   stile *[step]

subdued

suberb   suburb *[town]
                superb *[great]

subject

submarine   submariner

submerge [submerged]

submurje   submerge

subset

substance

substantial   substantially

substence   substance

substitute   substitution
  [substituting substituted]

subtract   subtraction
  [subtracting subtracted]

suburb   suburban   suburbia

subzero

succeed [succeeding succeeded]

success   successes

successful   successfully

such

suck [sucking sucked]

sucseed   succeed

sucsess   success

suction

sudden   suddenly

sudenley   suddenly

suede *[leather]   swayed *[moved]

sueur   sewer *[drain]

          sure *[certain]

suffer   sufferer

   [suffering suffered]

sufficient   sufficiently

suffix   suffixes

suffocate   suffocation

   [suffocating suffocated]

suffragette

sufishent   sufficient

sufokate   suffocate

sugar   sugary

suggest [suggesting suggested]

suggestion

suit

suitable   suitably

sulen   sullen

sulk [sulking sulked] sulkily

sulky   sulkier   sulkiest

sullen   sullenly   sullenness

sultan

sultana

sum *[add]   some *[amount]

sumer   summer

sumersorlt   somersault

sumery   summary
          *[short]
          summery
          *[warm]

summarise [summarised]

summary   summery
   *[outline]   *[warm]

summer   summertime

summit

sumthing   something

sun *[shine]   son *[boy]

sun   ~bathe ~burn ~burnt

sun   ~flower ~glasses ~lit

sun   ~light ~rise ~screen

sun   ~set ~shine ~stroke

sun   ~tan ~tanned

sundae *[ice cream]

Sunday *[day of week]

sune   soon

sung

sunk   sunken

sunny   sunnier   sunniest

super *[fab]   supper *[meal]

superb   superbly

superhero

superhuman

superior   superiority

supermarket

supersonic

supervise   supervisor

[supervising supervised]

supervision

suply   supply

suport   support

supose   suppose

supper *[meal]   super *[fab]

suppervise   supervise

supply   supplies

[supplying supplied]

support   supportive

[supporting supported]

suppose   supposedly

[supposing supposed]

supprise   surprise

sure *[certain]   shore *[sea]

surely

surender   surrender

surf *[sea]   serf *[slave]

surface   surfaces

[surfacing surfaced]

surge [surging surged]

surgeon

surgery   surgeries

surgical   surgically

surly

surmon   sermon

surname

suround   surround

surpent   serpent

surpliing   supplying

surprise   surprisingly

[surprising surprised]

surrender   surrendered

surround   surroundings

[surrounding surrounded]

survalence   surveillance

survant   servant

surve   serve

surveillance

survey   surveyor

[surveying surveyed]

survice   service

surviet   serviette

survival   survivor

survive [surviving survived]

suspect [suspecting suspected]

suspend [suspended]

suspense

suspicion   suspicious

suspiciously

sutch   such

sute   soot *[coal]

               suit *[clothes]

sutibul   suitable

suvenear   souvenir

swade   suede

swagger [swaggering swaggered]

swallow   swallowed

swam

swamp   swamped   swampy

swan [swanning swanned]

swap [swapping swapped]

swarm *[bees]   swam *[swim]

swat *[hit]   swot *[study]

sway [swaying swayed]

swayd   suede

sweat *[hot]   sweet *[food]

   [sweating sweated]

sweater

sweaty   sweatier   sweatiest

swede *[vegetable]

Swede *[from Sweden]

sweep   sweeper [sweeping swept]

sweet   sweetly   sweetness

sweeten sweetened sweetener

swept

swerve [swerving swerved]

swet   sweat *[hot]

               sweet *[food]

swetter   sweater

swich   switch

swift   swiftly   swiftness

swim   swimmer

   [swimming swam swum]

swine

swing

swipe [swiping swiped]

switch [switches switching switched]

swivel [swivelling swivelled]

swollen

swollow   swallow

swomp   swamp

swon   swan

swoop [swooping swooped]

swop   swap

sword   ~fish ~sman

swot *[study]   swat *[hit]

swum

swung

swurve   swerve

swyne   swine

swype   swipe

sycul	cycle

Check out cy as well

syclist	cyclist
syclone	cyclone
sygn	sign
sylens	silence
sylent	silent
sylinder	cylinder
syllable	syllabic
syllabus	
symbol *[sign]	cymbal *[music]

symmetrical
sympathetic   sympathetically
sympathise
   [sympathising sympathised]
sympathy

syncere	sincere
synonym	
syrup	syrupy
systematic	systematically
syte	cite *[quote]
	sight *[seeing]
	site *[place]

T-shirt

tabby

tabel   table

tabelspoon   tablespoon

table   tablecloth

tablespoon   tablespoonful

tablet

tabloid

tac   take

tack *[nail]   take *[get]

tackle [tackling tackled]

tacks *[pins]   tax *[money]

tacky   tackier   tackiest

tact   tactful   tactfully

tactic   tactical

tactless   tactlessly

tadpole

taek   take

tag [tagging tagged]

t'ai chi

tail *[dog]   tale *[story]

taip   tape

tair   tear

take [taking took taken]

takeaway   takeover

takul   tackle

taks   tax

taksi   taxi

takt   tact

taktik   tactic

tale *[story]   tail *[dog]

talen   talon

talent   talented

talk [talking talked]

talkative

tall   taller   tallest

talon

tame [taming tamed]

tamper [tampering tampered]

tan [tanning tanned]

tang   tangy

tangerine

tangle [tangled]

tanjerine   tangerine

tank

tannoy

tantrum

tap [tapping tapped]

tap-dance   tap-dancing

tape [taping taped]

tapestry   tapestries

tapistry   tapestry

tar [tarred]

tarantula

target [targeting targeted]

tarmac

tarnish [tarnished]

tart   tartness

tartan

task [tasked]

tassel [tasselled]

taste [tasting tasted]

tasteful   tastefully

tasty   tastier   tastiest

tattered   tatters

tattoo   tattoos

tatty   tattier   tattiest

tatu   tattoo

taught *[teach]   taut *[tight]

taunt [taunting taunted]

Taurus

taut *[tight]   taught *[teach]

tawn   torn

tawny

tax [taxes taxing taxed]

taxi   taxis

tea *[drink]   tee *[golf]

teach [teaches teaching taught]

teacher

team *[group]   teem *[swarm]

teanage   teenage

teapot   teaspoon   teatowel

tear *[cry]   tier *[layer]

tear *[rip] [tearing torn]

tearful   tearfully

tease [teasing teased]

Teashert   T-shirt

teaspoon   teaspoonful

techer   teacher

technical   technically

technician

technique

technology

teddy   teddies

tedious

tedy   teddy

tee *[golf]   tea *[drink]

  [tees teeing teed]

teef   teeth

teejuncshun   T-junction

teem *[swarm]   team *[group]

teenage   teenager   teens

teese   tease

Teeshert   T-shirt

teespoon   teaspoon

teeter [teetering teetered]

teeth *[mouth]   teething

teethe *[grow teeth]

tef   teeth

tekneek   technique

tekst   text

telefone   telephone

telephone   telephonist
  [telephoning telephoned]
telescope   telescopic
televise [televised]
television
telivise   televise
telivizhun   television
tell [telling told]   teller   telltale
telly
temper   temperamental
temperature
temple
temporary
tempracher   temperature
tempramentl   temperamental
tempt [tempting tempted]
tempul   temple
tempur   temper
ten   tenth
tenant
tend [tended]   tendency
tender tenderly tenderness
tendon
tendur   tender
tenent   tenant
tener   tenner *[£10]
                  tenor *[sing]

tenner

tennis
tenor
tenpin bowling
tense [tensed]   tensely
tenshun   tension
tension
tent
tentacle
tenth
tepid
terban   turban
terer   terror
tererise   terrorise
tereybul   terrible
terier   terrier
terific   terrific
teriss   terrace
teritoriel   territorial
terkey   turkey
term [termed]
terminal   terminally
terminate   termination
  [terminating terminated]
termoil   turmoil

Check out
tur as well

terning   turning

212

ternip	turnip	tey	tea
terodactil	pterodactyl	thach	thatch
teror	terror	than	
terqwoys	turquoise		

Check out
F as well

terrace terraced		thank [thanking thanked]	
terracotta		thankful thankfully	
terrapin		thankless thanklessly	
terrestrial		thank you	
terrible terribly		that	
terrier		thatch [thatched]	
terrific terrifically		thaw [thawing thawed]	
terrify [terrifies]		thay	they
[terrifying terrified]		the	
territorial		theat	that
territory territories		theatre theatrical	
terror terrorism		theef	thief
terrorise terrorist		thees	these
[terrorising terrorised]		theft	
tertle	turtle	their *[own]	there *[place]
test [testing tested]		theirs *[owns]	there's *[there is]
testify [testifies testifying testified]		theis	these
tether [tethering tethered]		them themselves	
Tewder	Tudor	theme [themed]	
tewlip	tulip	then	
tewn	tune	theory theories	
Tewsday	Tuesday	ther	there
text [texting texted]			
texture			

213

therapy   therapist

there *[place]   their *[own]

they're *[they are]

therefore

there's *[there is] theirs *[owns]

therfour   therefore

thermometer

thers   there's *[there is]

                 theirs *[owns]

Thersday   Thursday

thes   these

these

they

they'd [they had, would]

they'll [they will, shall]

they're *[they   there *[place]

    are]   their *[own]

they've [they have]

thick   thicker   thickest

thicken [thickening thickened]

thicket

thickly   thickness

thief   thieves

thier   there *[place]

                 their *[own]

thigh

thik   thick

thimble   thimbleful

thin   thinner   thinnest

thing

think   thinker [thinking thought]

thinly   thinness

thir   their

third   thirdly

thirst   thirsty   thirstier

thirteen   thirteenth

thirty   thirtieth

this

thistle

thogh   though

thore   thaw

thorn   thorny   thornier

thorough   thoroughly

thoroughbred

thoroughness

thort   thought

thorteen   fourteen

thortless   thoughtless

those

though

thought   thought-provoking

thoughtful   thoughtfully

thoughtfulness

thoughtless   thoughtlessly

thoughtlessness

thousand   thousandth

thow   though

thowsand   thousand

thrash [thrashing thrashed]

thread   threadbare

  [threading threaded]

threat

threaten [threatening threatened]

thred   thread

three   three-dimensional

thret   threat

thretton   threaten

threw *[ball]   through *[via]

thrill [thrilling thrilled]

thrive [thriving thrived throve]

throat   throaty

throb [throbbing throbbed]

throne *[king]   thrown *[ball]

throng [thronging thronged]

throo   through

throttle [throttled]

through *[via]   threw *[ball]

throughout

throw *[ball]   through *[via]

  [throwing threw thrown]

thrown *[ball]   throne *[king]

thrush   thrushes

thrust [thrusting thrust]

thud [thudding thudded]

thum   thumb

thumb [thumbing thumbed]

thump [thumping thumped]

thunder   thundery

  [thundering thundered]

thurmometur   thermometer

Thursday

thus

thwart [thwarted]

thwort   thwart

thyme *[herb]   time *[clock]

tiara

tic *[twitch]   tick *[clock,

  [ticking ticked]   mark]

ticket

tickle   ticklish [tickling tickled]

tidal

tiddlywinks

tide *[sea]   tied *[up]

tidy   tidier   tidiest

tie *[up]   Thai *[Thailand]

tie [ties tying tied]

tie chee   t'ai chi

tied *[up]   tide *[sea]

tier *[layer]   tear *[cry]

                    tire *[sleep]

                    tyre *[wheel]

tifoon   typhoon

tifoyd   typhoid

tiger   tigress

tight   tighter   tightly

tighten [tightening tightened]

tik   tick

tikul   tickle

tile

till *[until, shop]

tilt [tilting tilted]

timber

time *[clock]   thyme *[herb]
   [timing timed]

time   ~less ~table

timid   timidity   timidly

tin   tinned

tinge [tinged]

tingle [tingling tingled]

tinker [tinkering tinkered]

tinkle [tinkling tinkled]

tinsel   tinselly

tint [tinting tinted]

tiny   tinier   tiniest

tip *[advice]   type *[sort]

tiperiter   typewriter

tipes   types

tipical   typical

tiptoe [tiptoeing tiptoed]

tirannosaurus   tyrannosaurus

tirant   tyrant

tire *[sleep]   tyre *[wheel]

tire [tiring tired]

tireless   tirelessly

tirn   turn

tirteen   thirteen

tishue   tissue

tissue

tit *[bird]   tight *[firm]

titbit

tite   tight

title [titled]

titter [tittering tittered]

tiyed   tired

to *[do]   too *[also]

     two *[number]

toad *[frog]   towed *[pulled]

toadstool

toan   tone

toast [toasted]

tobacco   tobacconist

toboggan
   [tobogganing tobogganed]

today

toddle [toddling toddled]   toddler

tode   toad *[frog]

     towed *[pulled]

todel   toddle

toe *[foot]   tow *[pull]

toffee   toffees

toga

together   togetherness

toil [toiling toiled]

toilet   toiletries

token

toksic   toxic

told

toled   told

tolerable   tolerably

tolerait   tolerate

tolerance   tolerant

tolerate [tolerating tolerated]

toll [tolling tolled]

tolrabul   tolerable

tom   ~boy ~cat

tomato   tomatoes

tomb   tombstone

tombola

tomeake   tummy ache

tommow   tomorrow

tomorrow

ton *[imperial]   tonne *[metric]

tone   toneless

tongs

tongue

tonic

tonight

tonne *[metric]   ton *[imperial]

tonsil   tonsilitis

too *[also]   to *[do]
                    two *[2]

tooc   took

toocan   toucan

toogever   together

took

tool   toolkit

toom   tomb

toopay   toupée

toot [tooting tooted]

tooth   ~ache ~brush

tooth   ~less ~paste ~pick

toothy

tootifrooti   tutti-frutti

top [topping topped]

topic   topical

topple [toppled]

topsy-turvy

torch   torchlight

torcher   torture

torist   tourist

tork   talk

torment   tormentor
   [tormenting tormented]

torn

tornado   tornadoes

tornament   tournament

torney   tawny

tornt   taunt

torpedo   torpedoes

   [torpedoing torpedoed]

torrent   torrential

Torrus   Taurus

tortoise   tortoiseshell

tortoys   tortoise

torture   torturer

   [torturing tortured]

tortuss   tortoise

Tory   Tories

toss [tossing tossed]

tost   toast

total   totally

totem pole

totter [tottering tottered]

toucan

touch [touches touching touched]

touchy   touchier   touchiest

tough   tougher   toughest

toughen [toughened]

toughness

toupée

tour *[journey]   tore *[rip]

tourist   touristy   tourism

tournament

Tousday   Tuesday

tow *[pull]   toe *[foot]

   [towing towed]

toward   towards

towed *[pulled]   toad *[frog]

towel   towelling

tower [towering towered]

towle   towel

town

toxic   toxin

toy

toylet   toilet

trabl   trouble

trace   traceable   tracing

track [tracking tracked]

tractor

trade [trading traded]

tradesman

tradishun   tradition

tradition   traditional

traffic

tragedy   tragedies

tragic   tragically

traid   trade

trail [trailing trailed]

train   trainer [training trained]

trais   trace
traitor
trajedy   tragedy
trajic   tragic
trak   track
trale   trail
tram
tramp [tramped]
trample [trampled]
trampoline   trampolining
trance
trane   train
tranquil   tranquility
tranquilliser [tranquillised]
transatlantic
transe   trance
transfer [transferring transferred]
transform   transformation
[transforming transformed]
transishun   transition
transition
translate   translation
[translating translated]
transmishun transmission
transmission
transmit [transmitted]
transparent   transparency
transplant [transplanted]

transport [transported]
trap [trapping trapped]
trapeze
trapezium   trapezoid
trash   trashed   trashy
trauma   traumatic
travel   traveller
  [travelling travelled]
travler   traveller
trawler
tray
traytor   traitor
treacherous   treacherously
treachery
treacle
tread [treading trod trodden]
treason   treasonable
treasure   treasurer
  [treasuring treasured]
treasury
treat [treating treated]
treatment
treaty   treaties
treble
trecherus   treacherous
trechery   treachery
tred   tread
tree   trees

treeo	trio
treet	treat
treety	treaty
trek [trekking trekked]	
tremble [trembling trembled]	
tremendous tremendously	
tremor	
trench trenches	
trend trendy trendier	
treshere	treasure
trespass trespasses	
trew	true
trewansy	truancy
trewly	truly
trewthful	truthful
trial	
triangle triangular	
triathlon	
tribal tribe tribes	
tributary tributaries	
tribute	
triceps	
trick [tricked] trickery	
trickle [trickling trickled]	
tricky trickier trickiest	
tricycle	
tried	
trifle	

triggard	triggered
trigger [triggered]	
triing	trying
trik	trick
trikel	trickle
trile	trial
trilogy	
trim [trimming trimmed]	
trio	
trip [tripping tripped]	
tripet	tripped
triple triplets	
triseps	triceps
triumph triumphant	
trivial	
troble	trouble
trod trodden	
trofee	trophy
troff	trough
troll	
trolley trollies	
trombone trombonist	
troop [trooping trooped]	
trophy trophies	
tropic tropical	
trorma	trauma
trot [trotting trotted]	
trouble [troubling troubled]	

troublemaker   troublesome

trough

trousers

trout

trowel

trowser   trouser

truancy   truant

trubbel   trouble

truce

truck   trucker   trucking

trudge [trudging trudged]

true

truj   trudge

truly

trumpet [trumpeted]

truncheon

trundle [trundling trundled]

trunk

trupeez   trapeze

trust [trusting trusted]

trustworthy   trusty

truth   truthful   truthfully

truthfulness

try [tries trying tried]

trycycle   tricycle

tryed   tried

tryumf   triumph

tsar   tsarina

T-shirt

tsunami   tsunamis

tub   tubby   tubbier

tube   tubular

tuberculosis

tuch   touch

tuck [tucking tucked]

tuct   tucked

Tudor

Tuesday

tuffen   toughen

tuft   tufted   tufty

tug [tugging tugged]

tuition

tuk   took *[take]

            tuck *[in]

tule   tool

tulip

tumble [tumbling tumbled]

tume   tomb

tummy   tummyache

tumour

tumy   tummy

tuna

tune [tuning tuned]

tuneful   tunefully

tung   tongue

tunic

tunnel tunneller
[tunnelling tunnelled]

tupay   toupée

turban

turbulence turbulent

turf [turfed]

turkey *[bird]

Turkey *[country] Turkish

turm   term

Check out
ter as well

turmoil

turn [turning turned]

turnip

turquoise

turrestrial   terrestrial

turret

turtle turtledove

Tusday   Tuesday

tusk

tussle [tussling tussled]

tuth   tooth

tutor tutorial

tutti-frutti

tuword   toward

twang [twanging twanged]

tweak [tweaking tweaked]

tweed tweedy

tweek   tweak

tweet [tweeting]

tweezers

twelth   twelfth

twelve twelfth

twente   twenty

twentieth

twenty twenty-first

twerl   twirl

twevl   twelve

twice

twiddle [twiddling twiddled]

twig [twigged]

twilight

twin *[two] [twinned]

twine *[string] [twined]

twinge [twinged]

twinkle [twinkling twinkled]

twirl [twirling twirled]

twise   twice

twist [twisting twisted]

twisty twistier twistiest

twit

twitch twitches twitchy
[twitching twitched]

twitter twittery
[twittering twittered]

two *[2]	to *[in order to]	typewriter typist
	too *[also, very]	[typing typed]
twurl	twirl	typhoon
twylight	twilight	typhoid
ty	tie	typical typically
tyara	tiara	tyrannise [tyrannised]
tyde	tide *[sea]	tyrannosaurus rex
	tied *[up]	tyrant
tying		tyre *[wheel] tire *[sleep]
tyme	time *[clock]	tytan tighten
	thyme *[herb]	
type		

Check out
ti as well

ubout	about
udder	
uftaer	after
ugane	again
ugh	
ugly uglier ugliest	
ule	Yule
uliteration	alliteration
ulser	ulcer
ultraviolet	
umbrella	
umpire *[game]	empire *[lands]
[umpired]	
unable	enable
*[not able]	*[to make able]
unacceptable	
unaccompanied	
unaccustomed	
unaided	
unappetising	
unarmed	
unaversil	universal
unavoidable	
unaware	
unbearable unbearably	
unbelievable unbelievably	
unblock [unblocking unblocked]	
uncertain uncertainly	

uncertainty
unchanged
uncivilised
uncle
unconscious unconsciously
unconsciousness
uncontrollable
uncontrollably
unconvincing
uncover [uncovering uncovered]
undecided
undeniable undeniably
under ~cover ~graduate
under ~ground ~growth ~hand
under ~neath ~study ~wear
underestimate
underline [underlined]
undermine [undermined]
understand
 [understanding understood]
understandable
understandably
undertake undertaker
 [undertaking undertook undertaken]
undesirable
undignified
undiniabel undeniable
undo [undoing undid undone]

undoubted   undoubtedly

undrinkable

unearth   unearthly
  [unearthing unearthed]

uneasy   uneasier

uneatable   uneaten

unecessary   unnecessary

uneducated

uneek   unique

unekspected   unexpected

unemotional

unemployable

unemployed   unemployment

unenthusiastic

unequal   unequally

unequalled

unerth   unearth

uneven   unevenly

unexciting

unexpected   unexpectedly

unfair   unfairly   unfairness

unfaithful

unfamiliar

unfashionable   unfashionably

unfernished   unfurnished

unfinished

unflattering

unforeseeable

unforgettable

unforgivable

unfortunate   unfortunately

unfrendly   unfriendly

unfriendly

unfurnished

ungarded   unguarded

ungrateful   ungratefully

unhappiness   unhappily

unhappy unhappier unhappiest

unhealthy   unhealthier

unheard of

unien   union

unicorn

uniform

unimaginable

unimportant

uninhabited

unintentional

unintentionally

unintresting   uninteresting

uninterested   uninteresting

union *[join]   onion *[veg]

Union Jack

unique   uniquely   uniqueness

unisex

unit

unite [uniting united]

unity

universal   universally

universe

university   universities

unjust   unjustly

unkind   unkinder   unkindest

unkindly   unkindness

unkle   uncle

unknown   unknowingly

unleaded

unless

unlike   unlikely

unlovable   unloved

unlucky   unluckiest

unmanned

unmarked

unmistakable   unmistakably

unmoved

unnatural   unnaturally

unnecessary

unnown   unknown

unpaid

unpleasant   unpleasantly

unpleasantness

unplug [unplugged]

unpopular   unpopularity

unprepared

unpripared   unprepared

unprotected

unraliabul   unreliable

unrap   unwrap

unravel [unravelling unravelled]

unreal   unrealistic

unreasonable   unreasonably

unreliable

unritten   unwritten

unruly   unrulier   unruliest

unscramble [unscrambled]

unscrew [unscrewing unscrewed]

unsed   unsaid

unseen

unselfish   unselfishly

unselfishness

unsertain   uncertain

unshakeable

unsientific   unscientific

unsightly

unsivilised   uncivilised

unskilled

unskrew   unscrew

unsociable

unsolved

unsoshabul   unsociable

unspeakable

unspoken

unsporting

unsteady   unsteadily

unsuccessful

unsuccessfully

unsuitable   unsuited

untidy   untidier   untidiest

untie [untying untied]

until

untold

untrustworthy

untruthful

unusable

unusual   unusually

unuther   another

unwelcome   unwelcoming

unwrap [unwrapping unwrapped]

unwritten

unyun   onion *[veg]
                 union *[flag]

unyvers   universe

unzip [unzipping unzipped]

up ~beat ~right

upbringing

upgrade [upgraded]

upheaval

upheval   upheaval

uplift [uplifting uplifted]

upon

upper

uprising

uprite   upright

uproar

upset [upsetting]

upshot

upside-down

upstairs

uptight

uptite   uptight

upward   upwards

upwood   upward

uranium

Uranus

urban

urchin

Urdu

ure   your

urge [urging urged]

urgent   urgently   urgency

urine

urly   early

Check out
ear as well

urn *[vase]   earn *[money]

urnest   earnest

Uropean   European

urth   earth

227

us

use [using used]   user

usable   usage

useful   usefully   usefulness

useless   uselessly

uselessness

userp   usurp

usher [ushering ushered]

uskt   asked

usual   usually

usurp [usurped]   usurper

utensil

uther   other

utmost

utter [uttering uttered]

utterly

uver   other

uvm   oven

uway   away

uze   use

uzual   usual

V-neck   V-necked

vacancy   vacancies

vacant   vacantly

vaccinate   vaccination
   [vaccinating vaccinated]

vacuum [vacuuming vacuumed]

vael   vale *[valley]
                         veil *[cloth]

vage   vague

vague   vaguely   vagueness

vain *[proud]   vein *[blood]
                         vane *[weather]

vaiporise   vaporise

vakansy   vacancy

vakant   vacant

vaksinate   vaccinate

vaksine   vaccine

vakuum   vacuum

valay   valley

valentine

valew   value

valley   valleys

valuable

value   values

valuntine   valentine

valve

valyu   value

vampire

van

vandal   vandalism

vandalise [vandalised]

vane *[weather]   vain *[proud]
                         vein *[blood]

vanilla

vanish [vanishing vanished]

vanity

vaper   vapour

vaporise [vaporised]

vapour

variable

varied

variety   varieties

various   variously

varnish [varnishing varnished]

varse   vase

vary *[change]   very *[much]
   [varying varied]

vase

vast   vastly   vastness

Vatican

vault

vayn   vain *[proud]
                         vane *[weather]
                         vein *[blood]

veal

vector

vegetable

vegetarian   veggie

vegetation

vegtabul   vegetable

vehicle

veikel   vehicle

veil *[cloth]   vale *[valley]

vein *[blood]   vain *[proud]

                  vane *[weather]

veiw   view

vejetabul   vegetable

vejetarian   vegetarian

velocity

velvet   velvety

vencher   venture

vendetta

vending machine

vendor

venew   venue

Venn diagram

venom   venomous

vent [venting vented]

ventilate [ventilating ventilated]

ventilation   ventilator

ventriloquist

venture [venturing ventured]

venue

venum   venom

Venus

veray   very

verb   verbal   verbally

verbalise

vercabulary   vocabulary

verdict

verge

veriety   variety

verius   various

vermin

verruca   verrucas

verse

verses *[poem]   versus *[against]

version

versus *[against]   verses *[poem]

vertebra   vertebrae

vertebrate

vertex   vertices

vertical   vertically

vertigo

vertu   virtue

vertual   virtual

vertuos   virtuous

very *[much]   vary *[change]

vessel

vest

vet   veterinary

veteran

veto   vetoes [vetoed]

via

vialens   violence

vibe   vibration

vibrate [vibrating vibrated]

vicar   vicarage

vice   vice-president

vice versa

vicious   viciously

victim

victimise [victimising victimised]

victor

Victorian

victorious   victoriously

victory   victories

video   videos

vidio   video

vielence   violence

view [viewing viewed]

vigger   vigour

vigilance

vigilant   vigilantly

vigorous   vigorously

vigour

vikar   vicar

Viking

viksen   vixen

viktim   victim

viktimise   victimise

vile

vilense   violence

vilige   village

villa

village   villager

villain   villainous   villainy

vinager   vinegar

vinaigrette

vine   vineyard

vinegar   vinegary

vintage

violence   violent   violently

violet

violin   violinist

viper

virb   verb

Check out **ver** as well

virge   verge

virgin

Virgo

virjin   virgin

virse   verse

virtual   virtually

virtue   virtuous

virus   viruses

visa

visable   visible

vishus   vicious

visible   visibility   visibly

vision

visit [visiting visited]

visitor

visor

visual   visually

visualise   visualisation
   [visualising visualised]

vital   vitality   vitally

vitamin

vivid   vividly   vividness

vixen

vniler   vanilla

voat   vote

vocabulary

vocal   vocalist   vocally

vocation   vocational

voice [voicing voiced]

void

vokabulary   vocabulary

volcano   volcanoes   volcanic

vole

volkano   volcano

volley   volleyball

volnteerd   volunteered

volt   voltage

volume

voluntary   voluntarily

volunteer [volunteered]

vomit [vomiting vomited]

vorlt   vault

vote [voting voted]

vouch   vouched   voucher

vow [vowing vowed]

vowel

voyage   voyager

voys   voice

vue   view

vulcher   vulture

vulgar

vulnerable

vulture

vunrabel   vulnerable

vurb   verb

Check out **ver** as well

vurge   verge

vurse   verse

vurtuel   virtual

vya   via

wack   whack

wacks   wax

wad *[pad]   wade *[water]

waddle [waddling waddled]

wade *[water]   weighed *[load]
  [wading waded]

wafer   wafer-thin

waffle

wag [wagging wagged]

wage [waging waged]

wager

waggle [waggling waggled]

wagon

waht   what

waid   wade *[water]
                        weighed *[load]

waifer   wafer

wail *[cry]   whale *[sea]
  [wailing wailed]

waist *[body]   waste *[misuse]

waist   ~band ~coat ~line

wait *[delay]   weight *[load]
  [waiting waited]

waiter   waitress

waiting room

waj   wage

wake [waking woke woken]

wakeful

waken [wakening wakened]

waks   wax

Wales *[place]   whales *[sea]

walk [walking walked]

walk   ~about ~over ~way

walker

walkie-talkie

wall [walled]

wallaby   wallabies

wallet

wallop [walloping walloped]

wallow [wallowing wallowed]

walnut

walrus   walruses

waltz   waltzes

wand

wander *[roam]   wonder *[think]
  [wandering wandered]

want [wanting wanted]

war *[battle]   wore *[dress]

war   ~fare ~like ~ship ~time

ward [warding warded]

warden

wardrobe

warehouse   [warehousing]

wares *[goods]   wears *[coat]

warm [warming warmed]

warm-hearted

warmth   warmly

warn *[alert]   worn *[old]
  [warning warned]

warren

warrior

wart   warthog

wary   warier   wariest

was

wash [washing washed]

wash   ~basin ~out ~room

washer   washing

wasn't [was not]

wasp   waspish

wastage

waste *[misuse]   waist *[body]

wasteful   wastefully

wasteland

watch [watches watching watched]

watch   ~dog ~man

watchful   watchfully

water [watering watered]

water   ~colour ~cress ~fall

water   ~front ~logged

water   ~melon ~side ~tight

waterproof [waterproofed]

water-ski   water-skiing

watery

watt *[power]   what *[?]

watter   water

wave [waving waved]

wave   ~band ~length

wavy   wavier   waviest

wax [waxes waxing waxed]

waxwork

way *[track]   weigh *[load]

waykn   waken

wayt   wait *[delay]

               weight *[load]

we *[us]   wee *[tiny]

weak *[feeble]   week *[7 days]

weaken

  [weakening weakened]

weaker   weakest

weakly *[feebly]   weekly
                 *[every week]

weakness

weal *[mark]   wheel *[car]

               we'll
                 *[we will, shall]

wealth

wealthy wealthier wealthiest

weapon

wear *[dress]   were *[be]

               where *[place]

               weir *[dam]

wearily   weariness

weard   weird

wears *[coat]   wares *[goods]

weary   wearier   weariest

weasel

weather *[sun, rain] whether *[if]
[weathering weathered]

weather-beaten

weave *[cloth]   we've *[we have]
[weaving wove woven]

webbed

we'd *[we had,   weed *[plant]
      would]

wed *[married]

wedding

Wedensday   Wednesday

wedge [wedging wedged]

Wednesday

weed *[plant]   we'd *[we had,
[weeding weeded]   would]

weedy   weedier   weediest

week *[7 days]   weak *[feeble]

weekend

weekly *[every week]
  weakly *[feebly]

weel   weal *[mark]
                  wheel *[car]

weep [weeping wept]

weesal   weasel

weet   wheat

weeze   wheeze

weigh *[load]   way *[track]

weight *[load]   wait *[delay]

weight   weightless

weightlessness

weight   ~lifter ~lifting

weight training

weild   wield

weir *[dam]   wear *[dress]

weird   weirder   weirdest

weirdly   weirdness

wej   wedge

welcome [welcoming welcomed]

weld [welding welded]

welfare

well   better   best

well-behaved

well-known

well-mannered

wellington boot

welth   wealth

wen   when

Wensday   Wednesday

went

wept

werd   weird *[strange]

                  word *[speech]

were *[be]   whirr *[sound]

we're *[we are]   weir *[dam]

weren't [were not]

werewolf   werewolves

werk   work

werl   whirl

werld   world

werr   were *[be]

                whirr *[sound]

west ~bound ~erly ~ern

westwards

wet [wetting wetted]

wet   wetness

wether   weather *[sun]

                whether *[if]

we've *[we have] weave *[cloth]

whack [whacking whacked]

whacks *[hits]   wax *[candle]

whale *[sea]   wail *[cry]

whaling

what *[?]   watt *[power]

what   whatever

whatsoever

wheat

wheel *[car]   weal *[mark]

  [wheeling wheeled]

wheel ~barrow ~chair

wheeze   wheezy

  [wheezing wheezed]

when   whenever

whent   went

wher   where

where *[place]   wear *[dress]

                were *[be]

whereabouts

whereas

whereupon

wherever

whether *[if]   weather

                    *[sun]

whey *[milk]   way *[track]

which *[?]   witch *[hag]

whichever

whiff

while   whilst

whim

whimper [whimpering whimpered]

whine *[moan]   wine *[drink]

whined *[moaned]   wind *[turn]

whip *[beat] [whipping whipped]

whippet

whirl [whirling whirled]

whirl   ~pool ~wind

whirr *[sound]   were *[be]

  [whirring whirred]

whisk [whisking whisked]

whisker   whiskery

whisper [whispering whispered]

whistle [whistling whistled]

white   whiter   whitest

whitish   whiteness

whiz [whizzes whizzing whizzed]

who *[?]   hew *[cut]

who'd *[who had, would]

whoever

whole *[full]   hole *[gap]

whole   ~food ~hearted ~meal

who'll *[who will]

wholly *[fully]   holy *[God]

                    holey *[holes]

whom   whomever

whood   would

whooping cough

whopper   whopping

who're *[who are]

who's *[who is, has]

whose *[belongs]

who've *[who have]

why

wi   why

wich   which *[?]

                witch *[hag]

wicked   wickeder   wickedest

wickedly   wickedness

wicket   ~keeper

wide   wider   widest

widely

widen [widening widened]

widespread

widow   widower

width

wield [wielding wielded]

wier   weir *[dam]

                    we're *[we are]

wierd   weird

wiery   weary

wife   wives

wig

wiggle [wiggling wiggled]

wiggly

wigwam

wikid   wicked

wild   wilder   wildest

wilderness   wildernesses

wildly   wildness

wilful   wilfully   wilfulness

will

willing   willingly   willingness

willow   willowy

wilt [wilting wilted]

wily   wilier   wiliest

wim	whim
wimen	women
wimper	whimper
win [winning won]	
wince [wincing winced]	
winch [winches]	
[winching winched]	
wind *[turn]	whined
[winding wound]	*[moaned]
wind *[air]	
wind ~fall ~mill ~pipe	
wind ~screen ~surfer	
window ~pane	
windy windier windiest	
wine *[drink]	whine *[moan]
wing [winged]	
wing wingspan	
wink [winking winked]	
winner winnings	
winter ~time	
wintry	
wipe [wiping wiped]	
wiper	
wire [wiring wired]	
wire wireless	
wirlwind	whirlwind
wisdom	
wise wiser wisest	

wisell	whistle
wisely	
wish [wishing wished]	
wishful wishfully	
wisk	whisk
	whisker
wisp wispy	
wisper	whisper
wistful wistfully	
wit	
witch *[hag]	which *[?]
witchcraft witches	
with within	
wither [withering withered]	
without	
witness [witnessed]	
witnesses	
witty wittier wittiest	
wizard wizardry	
wnet	went
wobble [wobbling wobbled]	
wobbly	
woch	watch

Check out
wa as well

wod	wad *[pad]
	word *[speech]

woffel	waffle
woft	waft
woke woken	
wolf wolves	
wollaby	wallaby
wollet	wallet
wollop	wallop
wollow	wallow
woltz	waltz
woman women	
womb	
won *[victory]	one *[number]
wond	wand
wonder *[think]	wander *[roam]
[wondering wondered]	
wonderful wonderfully	
wons	once
wont	want
won't *[will not]	
wood *[trees]	would *[would go]
wooded	
wooden	
woodlouse	
wood ~land ~pecker ~wind	
wood ~work ~worm	
wool woollen woolly	
woom	womb
wopper	whopper

wor	war *[battle]
	wore *[clothes]
word [wording worded]	
word-processor	
wordy wordier wordiest	
wore *[clothes] war *[hit]	
work [working worked]	
workable	
work ~load ~man ~shop	
workitorkie	walkie-talkie
worl	wall
worlrus	walrus
world worldwide	
World War I	
World War II	
worm [worming wormed]	
worn *[used] warn *[alert]	
worpt	warped
worrant	warrant
worrior	warrior
worry [worries worrying worried]	
wors	wars
worse worst	
worsen [worsening worsened]	
worship	
[worshipping worshipped]	
worst	
wort	wart

worter — water

worth — worthless — worthwhile

worthy — worthier — worthiest

wos — was

wosh — wash

wosnt — wasn't

wosp — wasp

wot — watt *[power]

what *[?]

wotch — watch

would *[would go] — wood *[trees]

wouldn't *[would not]

wound *[hurt]
  [wounding wounded]

wove — woven

wow

wownd — wound *[clock]

woz — was

wrap *[pack] — rap *[pop, knock]
  [wrapping wrapped]

wreath

wreck [wrecking wrecked]

wreckage

wren

wrench [wrenches]
  [wrenching wrenched]

wrestle — wrestler
  [wrestling wrestled]

wretch *[rogue] — retch *[sick]

wretched — wretches

wriggle [wriggling wriggled]

wriggly

wrighting — writing

Check out R as well

wring *[wet] — ring *[circle, bell]
  [wringing wrung]

wrinkle — wrinkled — wrinkly

wrist — wristwatch

write *[pen] — right *[exact]

rite *[act]

writer [writing wrote written]

writhe [writhing writhed]

wrong — wrongfully — wrongly

wronged

wrote *[text] — rote *[learn]

wrung — rung
  *[squeezed] — *[ladder, bell]

wry *[humour] — rye *[grain]

wryly

wu — woo

wud — wood *[trees]

would *[would go]

wuff — woof

wulf — wolf

wull	wool	wurld	world
wully	woolly	wurldwide	worldwide
wuman	woman	wurr	were *[we were late]
wume	womb		
wunder	wonder *[think]		whirr *[sound]
wurd	word	wuz	was
wuren't	weren't [were not]	wyde	wide
		wyfe	wife
wurk	work	wyle	while *[when]
wurl	whirl		wile *[trick]

X-ray   X-rays

 [x-raying x-rayed]

xma   eczema

Xmas

xylophone

Check out **ex** as well

yacht   yachting

yachtsman   yachtswoman

yak

yam

yank [yanking yanked]

yap [yapping yapped]

yard

yashmak

yaun   yawn

yawn [yawning yawned]

yeah

year   yearly

yeast

yeer   year

yeest   yeast

yeh   yeah

yeild   yield

yeld   yelled

yell [yelling yelled]

yellow   yellower   yellowest

yellowish

yelo   yellow

yelp [yelping yelped]

yen

yer   year

yere   year

yes

yesterday

yet

yeti

yew *[tree]   ewe *[sheep]
                     you *[person]

yews *[trees]   use *[apply]

yield [yielding yielded]

yippee

yoak   yoke *[round
                          neck]

                  yolk *[egg]

yodel [yodelling yodelled]

yoga

yogert   yoghurt

yoghurt

yolk *[egg]   yoke *[neck]

yoow   you

yorn   yawn

yors   yours

yorself   yourself

yot   yacht

you *[person]   yew *[tree]
                 ewe *[sheep]

you'd *[you had, would]

youf   youth

you'll *[you will]   Yule *[Xmas]

young   youngster

youniform   uniform

your *[owns]   you're *[you are]

yours faithfully

yours sincerely

yourself   yourselves

yous   use

you'sd   used

youth   youthful

youth hostel

you've *[you have]

yo-yo

yu   yew *[tree]

                    you *[person]

yud   you'd *[you had,
                                would]

Yule *[Xmas]   you'll *[you will]

yummy   yum-yum

yung   young

yunger   younger

yuse   use

yuth   youth

zap [zapping zapped]

zapper

zeal   zealous

zebra   zebra-crossing

zeel   zeal

zero   zeros

zest

zigzag

  [zigzagging zigzagged]

zilophone   xylophone

Zimmer™-frame

zinc

zip [zipping zipped]

ziro   zero

zoan   zone

zodiac

zombie

zone [zoning zoned]

zonked

zoo   zoo-keeper

Zoolu   Zulu

zoom [zooming zoomed]

zoom lens

zu   zoo

Zulu

zylofone   xylophone